I0753776

The Beggar Boy

Chasing Dreams During Turbulent Times – A Quest to Leave Poverty Behind

Blending Memoir, Mythology, and Religious Commentary

ASHOK KUMAR MD

The Beggar Boy

ISBN:
978-1-966235-12-5 (paperback)
978-1-966235-13-2 (hardback)
978-1-966235-14-9 (ebook)

Published by:

OMNIBOOK Co.
99 Wall Street, Suite 118
New York, NY 10005 USA
+1-866-216-9965
www.omnibook.org

For e-book purchase: Kindle on Amazon, Barnes and Noble
Book purchase: Amazon.com, Barnes & Noble, and www.omnibook.org

Omnibook titles may be purchased in bulk for educational, business, fund-raising, or sales promotional use. For more information please e-mail admin@omnibook.org

Special Dedication

To my mother, *Shanti*,
who sacrificed everything
and allowed me to chase my dreams,
and with the grace of God,
all fell into place.

To *India*, my motherland,
which empowered me
with the wings of medical education,
and to the U.S., my adopted home,
for providing me with an open sky
and an unlimited horizon
to fulfill my dreams.

Contents

PART 2

PREFACE

The story's origin is from a united India. Before the partition, India was home to Hindus, Muslims, Christians, and many other religious communities. This diverse and beautiful nation was prosperous and peaceful, characterized by a unique kind of harmony among its various religions.

Living in this peaceful environment, different religions explored not only the physical but also the metaphysical nature of humanity. India's symphony of diverse religions and social harmony started to unravel when the British Empire took over and colonized India. The British political doctrine — "Divide and Rule" — would have catastrophic consequences for a peaceful and prosperous nation. After years of peaceful protest, the British were forced to leave India; however, before leaving, the British partitioned India on purely religious grounds. A new nation: Pakistan was carved out for the Muslims, and the rest of India for the Hindus, Christians, and Sikhs. Many secular Muslims decided to stay and refused to migrate to Pakistan.

The British departure from India resulted in mass migration, bloodshed, and suffering for millions of innocent people. About 14.5 million people moved across the newly defined border between India and Pakistan. [DLE1.1]

The Beggar Boy's family was Hindu, and to save their lives, they had no other option but to migrate to India. The family moved to New India. The town and the people where the family settled were alien to them.

They left behind the ancestral farm and home. Their new home and its hot weather were alien to them.

The Beggar Boy's family's misfortune and suffering were collateral damage resulting from the calculated political doctrine imposed on India by so-called highly civilized people.

The book is divided into two sections. The first section provides a kaleidoscopic view of Hindu civilization in India before the arrival of Muslims and the British. This section briefly discusses the Hindu religion and mythology and explains the contributions of Hindu scriptures to philosophy, quantum physics, and the deep analysis of metaphysical issues facing humanity.

This section also explains how a highly advanced and prosperous nation was humiliated and degraded to bone-crushing poverty and made a basket case by the British Empire. Despite the best efforts of the British, India survived as a democratic nation. It survived wars, famines, and became self-sufficient to feed its people. It became the fourth-largest economy in the world. [DLE2.1]

The second section of this book deals with the struggles and sufferings of a beggar boy's family after migrating to India. It tells the story of survival and the journey of a beggar boy to fulfill his destiny. The destiny of a nation and its people depends on who we are, what we struggle with, and what we achieve.

I believe you can't know who you are unless you know how to tell a story about yourself. "A man is always a teller of tales," the philosopher Jean-Paul Sartre observed. "He lives surrounded by his stories and the stories of others; he sees everything that happens to him through them, and he tries to live his own life as if he were telling a story."

The Beggar Boy is the story of my life, the story of my adopted home, the U.S., and its people. Without their life stories, my story would have been incomplete.

PART 1

INDIA – THE CRADLE OF ANCIENT CIVILIZATION

India's extraordinary geography is tied to its history. The meeting ground between East and West, India's geographical position made it a natural cradle of civilization. God blessed India with natural isolation, coupled with fertile land.

India is an inverse triangle protected in the North by the Himalaya Mountains and in the West by the Hindukush mountain range. It is a miniature world by itself. The mountain farming walls are in the North and West, and the Indian Ocean is a moat on all other sides. India's geography was the envy of many nations. It was nature's gift to humanity—a secure abode to develop. Before the arrival of the British, India developed materially, physically, and spiritually.

The first wave of globalization occurred when India's exports began to flow through the Golden Road. Commerce between India's west coast and the Roman Empire in Egypt started in the first century. Subsequently, in the 5th and 6th centuries, India started trading with Southeast Asia. Buddhism from India spread to China in the 7th century. For a brief period, there was an Indianization of the royal court.

By the 13th century, India's mathematical and astronomical ideas reached Europe through the Arab world.

For a millennia and a half, India was a confident exporter of its diverse civilization, creating a vast empire of ideas around it. India's art, religions, technology, astronomy, music, dance, literature, mathematics, and mythology blazed a trail across the world, along a Golden Road that stretched from the Red Sea to the Pacific. Indian ideas and religious insights are among the crucial foundations of our world. Ancient India provided profound answers to the big questions about the world—how it operates, why we are here, and how we should live our lives.

"In matters of science, astronomy and mathematics, India was to be a teacher of the Arab world and hence Mediterranean Europe too."
— William Dalrymple

The Mongol conquests in the 13th and 14th centuries in Asia ended India's centrality in world commerce, paving the way for the emergence of the Silk Road.

Thanks to the winds of the Asian monsoon, India became one of the largest economies in the world. India lies at the center of a great network of navigable sea roads and maritime trade routes.

In early summer, the heating of the Tibetan Plateau creates an area of low pressure that draws the moist, calm winds from the Bay of Bengal. Every winter, cold air rakes out from the snows of the Himalayas to the warm seas beyond.

The Indian Peninsula sits at the center of the vortex of winds, which blow one way for six months of the year and then reverse themselves for the next six months. The regularity and predictability of winds generate monsoons, which have enabled Indian sailors for millennia to raise their sails and propel themselves across the ocean at speed, then safely return home when the winds reverse.

Early Indian traders utilized the sea routes of monsoon Asia to travel in both directions. Many headed westward on the winter winds to the east coast of Africa and the rich kingdoms of Ethiopia. Here, the traders had a choice: one northern fork led through the Persian Gulf to Iran and Mesopotamia, while the other, to its south via Aden, took them to the Red Sea and Egypt.

Indian traders heading west used to arrive with the trade winds in early summer and ride the summer monsoon home with the winds behind them. The journey from the mouth of the Red Sea to Gujarat could take as little as 40 days, though if you missed the winds, the round trip might take as long as a year.

These unique wind vortices created a superhighway in the sea on which not only Indian merchandise but also its culture traveled to the rest of the world.

Sadly, India's contributions to the evolution of the ancient world are forgotten. The world is familiar with the Silk Road and its significant contributions to global commerce. Before the Silk Road, India's Golden Road and its unique navigable sea winds were the backbone of world prosperity.

From the end of the first millennium B.C. to the beginning of British rule in India, India's share of global industrial output was 25% in 1750. According to evidence cited by historian Immanuel Wallerstein, per capita agricultural output and consumption standards in 17th-century India were higher than in 17th-century Europe and early 20th-century British India.

In the 18th century, India was the most important manufacturing hub for international trade, with key industries including textiles, shipbuilding, and steel. The state of Bengal generated 12% of the world's GDP. Before British colonial rule, India was a thriving hub for agricultural and industrial goods. The world fondly called India "The Golden Bird."

Ancient India was where the rest of the world came to get rich through commerce and trade. The Persians, Greeks, Chinese, nomads, Arabs, Portuguese, and British came to India, seeking this metaphorical golden bird, to become rich. The alien traders were able to take some parts of "The Golden Bird" but were unsuccessful in killing "The Bird"; the soul of the Golden Bird—India—survived. Hindu mythology, religion, and culture survived these aliens and their inhuman behavior. India humanized these barbarians by teaching them the concept of meditation and the art of Yoga. Their belief in the monotheistic concept of God was shattered when they read and understood the Vedas and their teachings on the "Inclusive God."

Aldous Huxley was an English writer and philosopher who was nominated for the Nobel Prize nine times. After studying and understanding Hindu scriptures, he wrote the famous book *The Perennial Philosophy*. He elaborates the Sanskrit formula *Tat Tvam Asi* ("That art thou"): the *Atman*, or immanent eternal Self, is one with *Brahman* (the ultimate reality). The Absolute Principle of all existence—and the final search of every human being—is to discover the facts for himself, to find out who he is.

The greatest German speculative mystic, Meister Eckhart, wrote, "The more God is in all things, the more He is outside them, the more He is within, the more without." Pope John XXII accused him of heresy and tried him as a heretic. He died before the verdict was implemented.

The Greek, Roman, and Egyptian mythologies died with the rise of Christianity and Islam. Despite countless assaults and massive destruction of places of worship, the Hindu religion and mythology not only survived these assaults but are also very much alive and flourishing both in India and Nepal.

The Vedas extensively debated and discussed the concept of God, the Ultimate Reality, Brahman, and its different manifestations. Cultures often spread from one nation to another through cultural diffusion, which is the transfer of any element of a culture from one group to a group that does not already possess that element in its own culture.

Commerce between India and the rest of the world led to the exchange of goods, ideas, and cultural customs. For example, Buddhism, one of the religions of the Kushan Kingdom, reached China. With merchants' caravans, Buddhist monks went from India to Central Asia and China, preaching the new religion.

Along with Indian spices and silk, the Greeks also learned Hindu scriptures and their gods. Commerce and culture go hand in hand. In ancient India, a unique fusion of culture and commerce existed.

The Hindu gods were often depicted as Greek gods with Greek names.

The god Indra became Zeus. Indra and Zeus were assigned specific responsibilities: to be the kings of the gods. Both were blessed with a special, powerful thunderbolt to solidify their hierarchy, and both slew sea monsters.

The Hindu god Yama became the Greek god Hades. Both lords over death preside over the nether world (the world of the dead), and both decide the fate of the souls that pass their realm.

Sharvara and Cerberus are the hounds of hell. Sharvara was Yama's hound, and in Greek mythology, Cerberus was depicted accompanying Hades. The hounds guard the gates of their respective nether worlds.

Lord Krishna and Achilles: Both were killed by arrows piercing their feet—the only vulnerable part of their bodies.

Sita and Persephone: In Greek mythology, Persephone is known as Kore. She was abducted by Hades and became the queen of the netherworld. In Hindu mythology, Sita was also abducted. Both Sita and Persephone disappeared under the earth.

Kama Deva and Cupid: Gods of love and desire, both shoot arrows into the hearts of unsuspecting people to make them fall in love.

Mount Kailash and Mount Olympus: Both are real mountains. Mount Kailash is home to Lord Shiva, and Mount Olympus is home to the twelve Olympian gods.

Indian and Greek philosophies have made significant contributions to the modern philosophies we know today. The Indian influence on Greek philosophy is debated, and numerous controversies exist regarding whether the Vedas and Upanishads (Hindu scriptures) contributed to the development of modern Greek philosophy.

The Vedas

The Vedas, a Sanskrit word meaning *Knowledge* and *Wisdom*, are a large body of religious texts originating in ancient India. They are the oldest scriptures of Hinduism. While the Vedas prescribe rituals to appease deities, the Upanishads are concerned with the nature of reality, mind, and self.

1. There are four Vedas, the oldest of which is the Rig Veda. It was composed between 1500 and 1200 BCE, and the three Vedas—the Yajur Veda, Sama Veda, and Atharva Veda—were composed between 1200 and 900 BCE. There are 20,374 mantras in all the Vedas.

Each Veda has four sections, and the last section is called Vedanta. It combines *Veda* (knowledge) and *Anta*, which means end. It is also called the Upanishads. Each Veda has a varied number of Upanishads. In total, there are 12 major (Mukhia) Upanishads. They were composed between 800 and 300 BCE.

All Upanishads aim to investigate the ground of all Beings, pulsating with an underlying essence called

Atma (Self), and the relationship between *Atma* and *Brahman*. In the Upanishads, we note for the first time the emergence of central concepts of Hinduism. Such concepts include the doctrine of rebirth, the law of Karma, and mental training such as meditation and yoga.

It is the Upanishads that have guided and continue to influence the lives and thoughts of millions of Hindus.

As Patrick Olivelle writes - *The Upanishads are the Vedic scriptures par excellence of Hinduism.*

Katha Upanishad & Plato's Phaedo

This section highlights the similarities between the Vedic scriptures and Greek philosophy.

The *Katha Upanishad*, composed around 300 BCE, is the third-longest Upanishad of the *Yajurveda*. It deals with the secret of death and the separateness of the body and the *Atma* (Self).

The following are dialogues between Nachiketa, a curious young man searching for the secret of death, and Yama (King of Death).

Nachiketa asks Yama, the King of Death, "When a person dies, this doubt arises: he still exists, and others say he does not. O King of Death, dispel this doubt of mine. Does a person live after death or does he not?"

The King of Death says, "When a person identifies himself with his body, he will not be able to understand the secret of death. However, under the guidance of an enlightened teacher, he can learn how to dissociate himself from his physical identity. The path to understanding this secret is painful and difficult—just like walking on the razor's edge." Yama discourages

Nachiketa, advising him to go back and enjoy his material wealth, but Nachiketa insists that he will not return until he learns the secret of death.

Yama tells Nachiketa that the human body is a chariot. The horses pulling the chariot are our countless desires. The intellect is the charioteer; our mind holds the reins to keep desires under control. The most important component of this chariot is the rider—the Self. The Self is different from the body. Once a person understands the separateness of the body and the Self (*Atma*), they will understand the secret of death.

Yama teaches Nachiketa five levels of meditation:

1. Body senses
2. Mind
3. Intellect
4. Ego
5. Self

Once you reach an ego-free state through the discipline of meditation, the fear of death disappears, and an individual transcends his identification with the body.

Once the ego-free life is lived, the mortal becomes immortal. With the discipline of meditation, the duality between the Self and *Brahman* disappears. The *Atma* (Self) merges with *Brahman* (the ultimate reality) and becomes immortal.

The *Bhagavad Gita* is a 700-verse Hindu scripture written in Sanskrit. In Hinduism, time is non-linear.

The great god is involved not only in creation but also in dissolution.

In verse 32, death literally translates as "World-Destroying Time." The *Gita* says that death is an illusion, that we are not born, and that we don't die. According to this philosophy, there is only one consciousness, and the whole creation is a wonderful play.

Plato's Phaedo

The Phaedo is one of the most widely read dialogues written by the ancient Greek philosopher Plato. It is a conversation between Socrates and his friend Phaedo, an interlocutor, on the day of Socrates' execution.

Socrates called himself a gadfly and a midwife, refuting his interlocutors' falsehoods and helping them bring true ideas into being. Refutation was never to be done for its own sake; only by helping to peel the scales from people's eyes could they see the world anew. Socrates was known to challenge his interlocutors to the point of exasperation.

He believed that acts of destruction and creation are connected, and that the journey to reach the core of an idea begins with negation.

Socrates believed that thinking was a communal process: "In the presence of others, something becomes possible that is not possible when you are alone."

He said, "I realized, to my sorrow and alarm, that I was getting unpopular." He had alienated a few powerful politicians in Athens.

At the age of 71, Socrates was sentenced to death by being made to drink poisonous hemlock. His crime was preaching philosophy. One of the topics discussed in *Phaedo* is the immortality of the soul. Socrates taught his followers the distinction between body and self (or soul). The body decays and ages, but the soul is indestructible. For a person who identifies with the physical body, death is a hard reality; but for one who identifies as part of cosmic consciousness, death is an illusion.

On the question of death, the soul, and the afterlife, Socrates says, "I desire to prove to you that the real philosopher has reasons to be cheerful when he is about to die. After death, he may be able to obtain the greatest goods in the other world. The man can attain real wisdom after death. This life is full of distractions—life's distractions take away the power of thinking in us."

Our visible self bears an affinity with the invisible. Just as fire will never bring cold, the soul—the bringer of life—will never bring death. We are not purely a physical system, because we possess free will.

In conclusion:

The *Katha Upanishad*, *Bhagavad Gita*, Plato's *Phaedo*, and *The Perennial Philosophy* by Aldous Huxley discuss the nature of the Ultimate Reality (*Brahman*). We are part of Cosmic Consciousness and not separate from it—*Tat Tvam Asi*, meaning "you are Being itself," "you are Reality itself," "you are Existence itself." You are the *Atma* = you are the *Brahman*. Once we understand this concept, the fear of death—and death itself—become irrelevant.

Since the Upanishads were written (800–300 BCE), well before Socrates' time, I believe that the basis of Greek philosophical concepts was the Upanishads. Along with exporting spices and silk, India enlightened the world with numerous metaphysical concepts.

Science takes us up to the "Big Bang," but beyond that, we need different tools that India provided to humanity.

India's Contribution to Mathematics

Mathematics has been described as the longest continuous human thought. Albert Einstein said, "Mathematics is the poetry of logical ideas."

The Western narrative is that mathematics originated in Greece, but India's contribution to the field of mathematics dates back much earlier than Greece. This West is labeled as barbarian science. A racial and derogatory term, *ethnomathematics,* was invented to describe India's contribution. Indian mathematicians were more advanced than their Western counterparts. The logical ideas to solve intricate mathematical problems were in their DNA.

India gave the ancient world crucial mathematical concepts, such as zero, and the very form of numbers we all use today. This is arguably the closest thing humanity has to a universal language.

Mathematics is the universal language that allows us to understand and navigate the intricacies of the world around us.

Galileo Galilei said, "Mathematics is the language God has written the universe in." In other words, Galileo meant to say that the universe cannot be read until we have learned the language of mathematics and become familiar with its characters.

The invention of zero by the Indian mathematician Aryabhata introduced this remarkable contribution in the 5th century AD. Brahmagupta, an astronomer and mathematician, used zero in mathematical operations such as subtraction and addition. He introduced the concept of zero in calculations around 628 AD. This invention outweighs all others by any other nation, since it is the basis of the decimal number system, without which no advancement in mathematics would have been possible.

The invention of calculus is traditionally attributed to Isaac Newton and Gottfried Leibniz, who worked independently in the 17th century. However, it is incorrect to attribute the origin of calculus solely to Western civilization, claiming that it lies with either Leibniz or Newton. Instead, some claim that calculus originated in India in the 14th century with a mathematician named Madhava. Madhava taught at a school in Kerala, India.

An Indian mathematician, George Geevarghese Joseph, in his book *A Passage to Infinity*, argues that there was a pathway for knowledge from India to the West. This suggests that the school could have influenced Newton and Leibniz from Kerala.

As we know, ancient India was a wealthy nation, and practically all other nations traded with it. The exchange of goods, ideas, and culture between nations was constant. The history of cultural diffusion started with the Golden and Silk Roads, which ran from China to Europe.

Perhaps the European sailors used Madhava's work in navigation. It might then have been absorbed into European practices without anyone knowing, centuries later, its origin. This would be the case: someone told someone, who told someone, who told someone, and so on—more than 600 years ago.

Srinivasa Ramanujan was a self-taught mathematician whose suppositions were so profound and wide-ranging that their implications are still being considered.

In the 1890s, the Indian biologist J.C. Bose attempted to study the electricity in plants. He was known as the pioneer of wireless telecommunication, having discovered millimeter-length electromagnetic waves—the microwaves that made the first radios possible and are used in remote-sensing airport security scanners today.

Bose had an embarrassing period when he dedicated a portion of his career to questioning whether machines were alive; when his scientific instruments began to slow down after repeated use, he saw a parallel to fatigue in human nerves. Alexander Graham Bell invented the telephone, but he was driven to do so by his belief that the static he could hear on the line were messages from dead people and might be coming from his dead brother.

Bell was not expunged from the canon, but Bose, being dark-skinned and Indian, lost his legacy and was forgotten by the Western world.
—The Light Eaters

During the time of colonization, India's countless contributions in the field of science became hostage to point-blank British racism.

India was home to the ancient Buddhist university Nalanda, with tens of thousands of learned monks—the Indian equivalent of the great Library of Alexandria. The university was nine stories high and contained three divisions: the *Ratnadhi* (the Sea of Jewels), the *Ratna Sagara* (the Ocean of Jewels), and the *Ratnaranjaka* (the Jewel-Adorned). The university dormitories housed the 10,000 monks and international scholars. They studied texts from different schools of Buddhism, as well as the sacred Vedas, logic, astronomy, metaphysics, mathematics, and the nature of reality.

Upanishads & Quantum Mechanics – The Convergence of Spirituality and Science

"Quantum mechanics, the crown jewel of our human evolution, the most accurate, far-ranging, and beautiful of all our physical theories. It lies behind the coming promise of godlike computing power. It has completely reshaped our world. We know how to use it; it works as if by some strange miracle. The mind can't come to grips with its paradoxes and contradictions. It is as if the theory had fallen to earth from another planet." — *When We Cease to Understand the World*

Nobody imagined that the spiritual epiphany experienced by Hindu civilization during the Vedic period would have a far-reaching effect on the evaluation of the field of physics. Before quantum physics, the classical theories of physics—Newton's *law of motion* and Einstein's *theory of relativity*—formed the bedrock of reality on which the world rested.

The philosophy of the Upanishads would become the mother of quantum physics—one of the most remarkable developments in the 20th century. Prominent European quantum physicists, including Erwin Schrödinger, Werner Heisenberg, and Albert Einstein, credited the Vedas with inspiring their quantum experiments.

Schrödinger extensively read Schopenhauer's writings, through whom he came to know the philosophy of Vedanta (Upanishads).

Niels Bohr and Erwin Schrödinger were avid readers of the Vedic texts and observed that their experiments in quantum physics were consistent with what they read in the Vedas. As Schrödinger said, "some blood transfusion from East to the West is needed to save Western science from spiritual anemia."

Werner Heisenberg said, "Quantum theory will not look ridiculous to people who have read Vedanta." While working on quantum theory, Heisenberg went to India to lecture and was a guest of Tagore. He spoke extensively with Tagore about Indian philosophy. These talks greatly aided him in his physics work, as they demonstrated that the new ideas in quantum physics were, in fact, not entirely unfounded. He realized that there was a whole culture that subscribed to very similar ideas. —As told to Erwin Schrödinger. Unpublished conversation

In quantum mechanics, the world we see is not reality but a projection onto our consciousness. As the Argentinian poet Jorge Luis Borges said, "Reality is something out there, independent of us, ubiquitous and durable in time."

Quantum theory will not look ridiculous to people who have read and understood the Upanishads.

In the Upanishads, quantum physicists found echoes of their theories.

It is an argument that the materialist model of classical physics, as a closed physical system in which electrons bounce around like billiard balls, has been overthrown by the quantum revolution, which demonstrates that probabilities only collapse into reality itself when a conscious mind is present to measure and observe. Quantum physics replaces this picture with wave-particle duality. Quantum physics insists that electrons don't behave like billiard balls but exhibit wave-particle duality, and this contradiction is the reality of quantum mechanics.

The *Tat-Tvam Asi* in quantum mechanics is the wave-particle duality, the universal reality of all particles. The *Tat-Tvam Asi* in the Upanishads is Body/*Atma* (Soul) = *Brahman*.

Every individual manifestation is only a reflection of *Brahman*, the absolute reality that underlies the world's phenomena; *Brahman* is the universal reality of this universe.

Holotropic breathing practice has been used for centuries by Hindus to promote emotional and spiritual well-being. One of the earliest forms of breathwork can be traced back to the ancient Indian practice of *Pranayama*. *Pranayama* is a Sanskrit word commonly translated to "breathing control," but it has a deeper meaning.

Prana translates to both life energy and breath; *Yama* means control, and *Ayama* means to lengthen. Its roots date back over 5,000 years. Ancient Hindu texts such as the *Upanishads* and the *Bhagavad Gita* discuss the importance of breathing control for spiritual growth and the attainment of a higher state of consciousness.

"Breathing Their Way to an Altered State" — *New York Times* article — discusses the psychedelic effect of deep abdominal breathing (holotropic breathing). According to Dr. Stanislav Grof, "this exercise had the potential to induce an altered state of consciousness so profound that the breathers have the capacity to heal themselves, relying less on medicine."

The demand for psychedelics as tools for healing has exploded in recent years. Many workshops in the state of Oregon and San Francisco are training health care professionals to guide patients through holotropic breathing treatment.

A God of philosophers and classical physicists is one thing, but the God of quantum physicists is just a bit too disreputable—at least until you have such an experience yourselves. Humanity does have a proper language to explain the quantum phenomenon.

In the coming years, humanity will see a unique fusion of quantum physics and the psychedelic effects of holotropic breathing. The duality between science and mysticism (spirituality) will become obsolete, which would be India's ultimate precious gift to humanity.

Mythology & Religion

When we do science, we are pantheists.
When we do poetry, we are polytheists.
When we moralize, we are monotheists.
— Goethe, Maxims and Reflections

Our mythology is more than mere stories. Mythology is as relevant to us today as it was to the ancients. It serves as a compass for each generation and finally becomes the core of its identity. It shapes the moral fabric of people, society, and the nation.

We ask: why are Hindu mythology and religion still alive and flourishing, while the mythologies of the Greek, Roman, Egyptian, and Norse have all faded away?

"In A.D. 302, Constantine started the process of Christianization of the Roman Empire, which reached its apex at the end of the 4th century when Theodosius I made Christianity the sole official religion of the Roman Empire.

For the Romans, the cross was a symbol of their power instead of a symbol of compassion, grace, and unconditional love. The Romanization of Christianity also changed the meaning of the cross.

The subsequent spread of Christianity across the Western world drove developments from the founding of cities to the framing of the idea of original sin to the suppression of religious diversity through violence.

The Constantinian conversion did not spiritualize the Roman Empire, but it was the Romanization of Christianity—the religion turning itself into a branch of the Roman state. The Romanization of Christianity would turbo-charge the dismantling of polytheistic beliefs." —*Pagan and Christian*, by Robin Lane Fox

Before the birth of Christianity and Islam, most of the world was polytheistic. There were numerous gods with specific healing powers. Monotheistic religions brought forth a new way of thinking and mindset about "Their God."

The main teaching of monotheistic religions is that there is only one God. This concept allayed a lot of confusion in people's minds. The power of the Roman Empire changed the philosophy of Christ's teachings. A humble and caring religion became arrogant and political. The teachings of Christ were interpreted through the prism of the unfettered power of the Roman Empire. The new mantra of Christianity—"Either my God or no God"—became the bone of contention, first between polytheistic religions and monotheistic Christianity, and later between Christianity and Islam.

The Ways of the Pagan

According to monotheistic religions, everything about polytheistic religions—rituals, places of worship, and their books—was considered demonic.

Deuteronomy, the fifth book of the *Torah*, preaches to believers to reject the ways of the pagan.

It says, "When you come into the land that the Lord your God is giving you, don't follow the disgusting practices of the nations that are there. Don't sacrifice your children in the fires of your altars; and don't let your people practice divination or look for omens or use spells or charms, and don't let them consult the spirits of the dead. In the land you are about to occupy, people follow the advice of those who practice divination and look for omens, but the Lord your God does not allow you to do this. Instead, he will send you a prophet like me (Moses) from your own people, and you are to obey him." *(Deuteronomy 18:9–22)*

As Saint Augustine said, "All the pagans' cultures are under the power of demons. Altars were set up to demons, priests ordained for the service of demons, sacrifices offered to demons. The ecstatic ravers were upgraded from prophets to demons."

To this end, Christian writers explained that the demons had created Hinduism and the Greco-Roman religious systems so that they might procure themselves a proper diet of fumes and blood offered to their statues and images. The temples of the old gods served as centers for demonic activities.

St. Augustine concluded, "Killing and burning people for the sake of our religion is ok with our 'Lord the Savior.'" —*The Darkening Age*, by Catherine Nixey

To justify the philosophy of "Either my God or no God," the Church started the religious war (Crusades), which would kill millions of innocent people.

In Alexandria and Rome, books of philosophy, arts, and music were burned while the Christian officials looked on in pride and satisfaction. Syrian bishop Rabbula advised his congregation to find pagan books and burn them. The houses of pagans were searched, and books dealing with rituals were vandalized and destroyed.

The philosophers were not allowed to teach or worship their gods. The great statue of Athena was torn down, and the treasures stored in temples suffered terribly.

The magnificent Parthenon temple was destroyed, and the library, which housed nearly 700,000 books, was burned. For over a month, books were burning in the streets of Athens.

The monotheistic religions' mantra of "Either my God or no God" will have catastrophic consequences for humanity. In India, the Hindu temples were destroyed, and to escape punishment from Muslim rulers, the Hindus started to pray at home. To this day, every Hindu home has a small temple in the house to pray. The core philosophy of Hinduism—that God is everywhere: you can destroy or take away my temple, but you cannot take away my God—helped them to survive the monotheistic onslaught on their religion.

> *"The conversion of the polytheistic world was an egregious example of the transvaluation of all values through Christianity, whereby the whole of the deified mode of life and thoughts of Greece, as well as the Roman Empire, were almost annihilated or transvalued in a comparatively short time."*
> *—Thus Spoke Zarathustra*

After destroying the Greco-Roman gods, their books, and temples, and to prove whose God is real, the Muslims and the Christians started religious wars with each other.

The Crusades: Religious Wars

Between 1096 and 1291, there were eight major Crusades. The Crusades were religious wars between Christians and Muslims. The main mission of these conflicts was to secure control of holy sites considered sacred to both Christians and Muslims.

The Crusaders suffered tremendous losses; historians estimate that only one in twenty Crusaders survived to reach the Holy Land. During the Crusades, 1.7 million people died. These deaths occurred at a time when the world population was 300 million, which is 420 million out of the present-day world population. —*Washington Post*, 2005/02/06

According to the *Encyclopedia of Wars*, out of all 1,763 known conflicts, 123—or 6.9%—have religion as their primary basis. The burning question in monotheistic religions is: Who is the true believer, and who decides? As we know, the arbiter of this question is monotheistic religions.

In the history of Homo sapiens' evolution, the concept of God came very late. Once the Sapiens harvested the wheat and became farmers, their survival became hostage to natural forces that were not under their control. The fear of starvation and mortality finally gave us the concept of God. This fear was exploited by organized religions to control and keep their followers in line.

The intriguing question we ask is: what is happening to the monotheistic religions? Technology has flattened our world, and in this new world, there is a constant exchange of ideas and diffusion of different political and religious belief systems.

When monotheistic religions invaded India and destroyed the places of worship, the world was not flat, and we were isolated from each other. Now, the fusion of different cultures is blurring the demarcation between monotheistic and polytheistic or non-monotheistic religions. The symphonies of monotheistic and polytheistic rituals are giving us a new religion: "Humanism."

Humanism values humans more than the divine or supernatural. It stresses the potential value and goodness of human beings, emphasize common needs, and seek only rational ways of solving human problems.

The original pagans were followers of ancient religions that worshipped several gods. Today, we say a person is pagan if he do not go to a synagogue, a church, or a mosque. So, in conclusion, if you are born a Christian and you do not go to church, you are a pagan.

The global population in 2022 is about 8 billion. There are 2.5 billion born Christians, 1.9 billion born

Muslims, and about 15 million born Jews. Out of the 8 billion world population, about half of the world is non-monotheistic, or you can call them pagans.

The modern definition of paganism is extremely broad; it includes rejection of strict monotheistic teachings, nature worship, agnostic and atheistic beliefs, and followers of Hinduism.

Evidence suggests that Americans are becoming significantly less religious. "We are currently experiencing the largest and fastest religious shift in the history of our country," Jim and Michael write in their book *The Great Dechurching*. The dechurching is apparent in all denominations. Some 40 million American adults once went to church but have stopped going, mostly in the past quarter-century.

As a Pew Research Center poll on religion revealed, in the millennial generation—which includes adult Americans under the age of 40—Christians are a minority. The share of self-identified Christians in the USA dropped to 63% in 2022 from 75% in 2011, while the share of religious "nones"—that is, those who identified as atheists, agnostics, or nothing in particular—jumped to 29% from 19%. The share of Republicans who belonged to a church was 65% in 2020, down from 75% in 2010. The Christian population has been shrinking over the past two decades. The changes are especially stark among the millennials. Pew Research Center issued a report noting that if the current trend continues, by 2070 the United States may no longer be a majority-Christian nation. —*Pew Research Center Study*

As noted by Davis and Graham, the Church has not seemed very Christian to many people. The guardians of Christianity—Rev. Jerry Falwell, Rev. Pat Robertson, and Jesse Helms—turbocharged the dechurching of America by suggesting that the HIV epidemic was God's punishment for promiscuity, and that the September 11 terrorist attacks on the World Trade Centers were God's lethal judgment on the behavior of feminists and gay people.

Humanism is coming without the Crusaders. Our humanistic core lifts the spirit and nurture empathy. Humanism comes in many flavors: Secular humanism, Christian Humanism, Jews Humanism, and so on. It deepens our understanding of the human hearts and makes other people seen, heard, and respected. The curtain of false narrative and calculated assaults on non-monotheistic ways of worship is coming off—whether the monotheistic hierarchy likes it or not.

Our humanistic core lifts the spirit and nurtures empathy. Humanism comes in many flavors: secular humanism, Christian humanism, Jewish humanism and so on. It deepens our understanding of the human heart and makes other other people seen, heard and respected.

At the core of our consciousness we are all seekers. We all want to know why. Man is asking animal. And while finding, the belief that we have found the answer can separate us and make us forget our humanity. It's the seeking that continues to bring us together, that makes and keeps us human. (The Seeker)

The *Rig Veda* is one of the four Vedas in Hinduism. It is the oldest Veda, and it discusses in great detail the fundamental question of our creator God and the creation of the universe; however, it does not categorically accept the existence of a creator God in many instances.

The monotheistic faith will stay, but humanized polytheism will replace monotheistic culture. In this new religion, religion and morality will be separated. In *Losing Our Religion*, Moore writes that the reason people leave churches is not that they lose their belief in God, but that they lose confidence in religious leaders and the Church's moral leadership.

The way to your God will not be through the golden gates of the Church or Synagogue. The importance of monotheistic rituals will diminish, and who is a true believer will be decided by the Almighty, not by the religious hierarchy.

Many people believe adoption of a polytheistic worldview would be beneficial for the world, replacing dominating orthodox monotheism, which they see as inherently repressive.

At the core of our consciousness we are all seekers. We all want to know why. Man is asking animal. And while the finding, the belief that we have found the answer, can separate us and make us forget our humanity.

It is the seeking that continues to bring us together, that makes and keeps us human.

The Crusaders of this new religion will change the world with true compassion, care, and love. God has blessed His children with free will; with this blessing, humanity will see the true nature and meaning of God.

The essence of spirituality is both ancient and timeless, regardless of the age of a specific religion. As the *Rig Veda* states, "When was it produced? Where is this creation? The gods came afterward with the creation of the universe."

Most people uphold their end of the bargain—religious institutions need to uphold theirs.

The British Foothold in India

The East India Company, an English and later British corporation, was founded in 1600 to trade in the Indian Ocean regions. At its peak, the company was the largest corporation in the world. The company had its own armed forces, totaling 260,000 soldiers—twice the size of the British army at the time.

The company's growth was phenomenal. During the mid-1700s and early 1800s, it accounted for half of the world's trade.

The East India Company ships docked at Surat in 1608. The company established its first factory in 1613 in Surat. Initially, the company struggled in the spice trade because of the competition from the well-established Dutch East India Company. The company decided to explore the feasibility of gaining a territorial foothold in mainland India.

The British understood the politically fragmented landscape of India better than other colonial powers. The country was ruled by many princely states fighting each other. The company requested that the Crown launch a diplomatic mission and approach the Mughal Empire. The British wanted to get their foot in the chaotic tent of Indian politics with the mission to take over the country by the political doctrine of divide and conquer.

The political doctrine of "Divide and Rule" that the British used to control their colonies was a time-tested strategy. Julius Caesar used it, rising to become one of the most powerful politicians in the Roman Empire. One of his senators, Marcus Junius Brutus, assassinated him.

In 1615, James I, King of Scotland and England, appointed Sir Thomas Roe, an English diplomat, as ambassador to represent England in the Mughal Empire. Sir Thomas Roe's mission was to arrange a commercial treaty between Britain and the Mughal Empire that would give the East India Company exclusive rights to reside and establish factories in Surat and other areas.

The Mughal emperor Nur-ud-din Salim Jahangir (Emperor of the World) ruled India from 1605 to 1627. He had a vast empire covering most of India. In exchange for a territorial concession, Sir Thomas Roe offered Emperor Jahangir goods and rarities from European markets. The mission was highly successful, and Jahangir sent the following letter to King James through Sir Thomas Roe:

The British presents selected for Emperor Jahangir included a scarlet cloak embroidered with silver, a velvet-covered chest of bottles with "hot water"—most likely Scotch from Scotland—several pictures, and the paintings of King James I, his queen Anne, East India Company governor Sir Thomas Smithe, and their ladies.

> *"Upon which assurance of your love, I have given my general command to all kingdoms and ports of my dominions to receive all the merchants of the English nation as subjects of my friend (King James I); that in what place soever they choose to live, they may have free liberty without any restrain, and at what port soever they shall arrive, that neither Portugal nor any other shall dare to molest their quiet. And in what city soever they shall have residence, I have commanded my governors and captains to give them freedom answerable to their desires, to sell, buy, and to transport to their own country at their pleasure.*
>
> *For confirmation of our love and friendship, I desire Your Majesty to command your merchants to bring in their ships all sorts of rarities and rich goods fit for my palace. You be pleased to send me your royal letters at every opportunity, so that I may rejoice in your health and prosperous affairs, that our friendship may be interchanged and eternal."*
>
> *—Nur-ud-din Salim Jahangir*
> *(Emperor of the World)*

Jahangir's agreement with the EIC would set the stage for the British to eventually take over the country. The British were able to exploit Jahangir's weakness for alcohol; he used to drink heavily and died of alcohol complications on 28 October 1627 at the age of 58.

Before the arrival of the East India Company, Portugal was the main European country doing business in India. Portuguese traders earned huge profits by selling and buying goods from India.

The fragmented politics and wars among Indian kings gave the British the golden opportunity to exploit the situation. Eventually, the Company became a dominant force in India's politics and wars. The East India Company once commanded a private army of 260,000 soldiers. This kind of military might gave the Company enough power to coerce Indian rulers into a one-sided contract that granted the Company lucrative taxation powers.

A major turning point in the East India Company's transformation from a profitable trading company into a full-fledged empire came after the Battle of Plassey in 1757. The battle pitted 50,000 Indian soldiers under the Nawab of Bengal against just 3,000 company men. The Nawab was angry with the Company for skirting taxes and was confident that he would kick the British out of India because of a huge manpower advantage. But the Nawab did not know that, behind his back, the British commander Robert Clive had struck a deal with Indian bankers not to supply funds for the war.

The Indian soldiers refused to fight at Plassey due to a lack of funds. This victory gave the Company broad taxation powers in Bengal, one of the richest provinces in India. (The province of Bengal generated 12% of the world's GDP in 1757.)

So, these two watershed events—Emperor Jahangir welcoming the British, and Indian bankers betraying the Nawab by helping Robert Clive—would change the fate of millions of Indians. These events paved the way for India's colonization, casting the land of Hindustan under 200 years of British rule.

In 1784, the British Parliament under Prime Minister William Pitt passed *The India Act*, which formally included the British Government in ruling over the East India Company's land holdings in India.

Nobody else to blame—the Indians gave away India to the British on silver and gold platters.

Eventually, British policies would reduce India from a highly advanced, economically vibrant, and proud nation to a poor basket case, struggling with starvation and famines.

In the 16th and 17th centuries, India had thriving cloth, metal, and carpentry industries. The British Raj forced local governments to import goods rather than produce locally. Before the British Raj, India's contribution to world GDP was 25%; it dropped to 0.3% when India became a free nation.

From a thriving industrial base, under the British Raj, Indian industries were reduced to supplying raw materials to British factories. British policies were designed to ensure that India remained undeveloped. While the rest of Europe and Japan were getting rich, no industrial revolution happened in India.

India had never experienced famines before the British. In the 16th and 17th centuries, the food consumption of an average Indian was much higher than that of a European. British agricultural policies created the worst famines in the 18th, 19th, and 20th centuries. The British encouraged—and in some cases, forced—Indian farmers to shift their focus and produce cash crops like cotton, sugarcane, and tobacco. These crops could not feed the local populations but were good for British tea houses and home decorations.

The change in agricultural policies led to 24 famines, killing millions between 1850 and 1899 alone.

The most startling case was the Bengal Famine in 1943, which killed up to 3 million people. It was a different kind of famine; we can call it a man-made disaster. There was no evidence of drought in late 1943, thought to be the peak of the famine. Rainfall levels were above normal.

According to Prof. Vimal Misra, "This was a unique famine, caused by policy failure instead of any monsoon failure." The decisions of Winston Churchill's wartime cabinet in London exacerbated the famine. When Indians were dying in large numbers, the British knowingly continued to export food from India to feed British soldiers fighting in Europe and Africa.

When Churchill was informed about the famine, he blamed the Indians and said, "Indians are breeding like rabbits," and asked how, if the shortage were bad, Mahatma Gandhi was still alive.

It is estimated that the British siphoned off $44.6 trillion (adjusted for inflation) from the Indian economy.

Apart from economic degradation, the British Empire was able to change the way Indians looked at and understood their religion, culture, and mythology. The British knew that to control the highly advanced culture of India, they would need more than brute physical force. By downgrading the Indian way of life and culture with a toxic narrative, the British were partially successful in changing India both physically and psychologically.

Our mythology is the basis on which we recognize ourselves as people. It gives us strength and holds us during crises. It is the core of our identity. By hijacking people's mythology, you take away and destroy their core identity.

Mythology has a coherent relationship not only with the past but also with the present. British psychologists understood this fundamental nature of the human psyche and exploited it to control their various colonies. The British created a virtual identity for Indians to the point where Indians started hating their own way of life and culture. An alternate reality was created, where a highly advanced religion (Hinduism) was labeled as primitive and backward, with pagan rituals.

The British in India created a smokescreen to hide tyranny, repression, and exploitation. The British were successful in destroying the Indian economy, but they were unable to destroy India's deep-rooted cultures, religions, and mythology.

The soul of India, the "Golden Bird," survived British repression. Its deep-rooted culture and religion have been reincarnated in a new, independent, vibrant India, where its mythology and culture are very much alive.

"In the coming future, India will recover its historical role as an economic powerhouse, and the past few centuries of poverty will be forgotten—a blink of an eye in the context of India's ancient civilization. It would be normal to think of India as a great power and one of the pillars of the global economy."
— New York Times, Op-Ed, by Nicholas Kristof

After destroying India's economy, the British were not done with India yet, and to finish the job, in 1947, the country was partitioned into two independent nations on religious grounds. The new nation of Pakistan, with a Muslim majority, was carved out of the Indian subcontinent, with the rest of the land going to the new independent secular India—home to a majority of Hindus and other minorities, including secular Muslims. This was accompanied by the largest migration of people on both sides of the border.

The task of demarcating the boundaries between the nations was given to a British lawyer, Sir Cyril Radcliffe, who had never been to India and was totally ignorant about Indian culture. Before partition, despite different religions, there was peaceful social integration between Hindus and Muslims in millions of small communities.

Sitting in England, Radcliffe drew the line on the map and divided the subcontinent. With this inhumane act, the British destroyed the social harmony and lives of millions of innocent people.

In an interview with journalist Kuldeep Nayyar in 1976 in Britain, Radcliffe said, "The time at my disposal was so short, and I could not do a better job. However, if I had two to three years, I might have improved on what I did." In a short period of five weeks, Radcliffe partitioned a country as diverse as India and sealed the fate of millions of people.

The British objectives were to create unrest and chaos and to show the world that the primitive people of India were not capable of taking care of their own affairs.

The British mission of physically destroying India was foiled by the vision of its founding father, Mahatma Gandhi's policies of inclusiveness and non-violence.

In one such poem about Sir Radcliffe, we see how fate decided who belonged and where.

He got down to working on the task of setting the fate of millions. The map at his disposal was out of date and the census return was almost certainly incorrect.

But there was no time to check them,
no time to inspect.
— W.H. Auden, "Partition"

The population of undivided India in 1947 was 390 million. After the partition, there were 330 million people in India, 30 million in West Pakistan, and 30 million in East Pakistan (now Bangladesh).

The partition of India unleashed an epic humanitarian crisis, and about 14.5 million people crossed the borders to what they hoped was the relative safety of their religious majority. Massive violence and killings occurred on both sides of the border. By some estimates, about 2 million deaths occurred.

I was 2 years old when the family crossed the border and migrated to New India. God's unconditional grace protected the family. They survived the heat, dust, starvation, and sectarian bloodbath. The new India where they migrated was as alien to them as going to a new planet in the solar system. It was not like the home they left behind in Pakistan—the landscape blushing with valleys and their beloved Jhelum River.

My father, mother, and sister would have stayed in Jhelum City in Pakistan. **Before** the partition of India, the family had been living there for centuries. The town is situated on the east bank of the Jhelum River. The town was named after the river, which is located between north-western India and north-eastern Pakistan in the province of Punjab. The city of Jhelum is known for providing soldiers to the British army; the city is also known as the City of Soldiers and the Land of Warriors.

The Jhelum River is believed to be "The Hydaspes" mentioned by Arrian (the historian for Alexander the Great). After conquering the Persian Empire, Alexander continued his journey to probe Northern India. In the year 326 BCE, Alexander the Great's campaign of conquest in Asia was stopped in Jhelum, the land of the warriors. This would be his last battle, also known as the Battle of Hydaspes or the Battle of Jhelum. It was the hardest, most brutal battle, where the Indian soldiers with rags and minimal armaments were able to stop him.

The Battle of Jhelum was fought between Alexander the Great and King Porus on the banks of the Jhelum River. In the end, after major losses on both sides, King Porus offered to surrender, and a large part of the province of Punjab, including the town of Jhelum, was absorbed into the Macedonian Empire.

The first meeting between Alexander the Great and King Porus was a unique and unconventional one between a victorious king and his vanquished foe. When Alexander asked how he wished to be treated, Porus replied, "Treat me as a king will treat another king." Impressed, Alexander indeed treated Porus like a king, allowing him to keep his land.

My dad and the people of Jhelum were proud that King Porus did not beg for his life and maintained his dignity even after a crushing defeat. The people of Jhelum knew their history and were proud of the fact that they stopped Alexander the Great from invading the rest of India. The first meeting between Alexander and Porus became the subject of many plays shown in schools all over the province of Punjab.

Alexander's army, exhausted after the Battle of Jhelum, demanded they be allowed to return to the West. A Hindu Naga Sadhu from Jhelum, whom the Greeks called Calanus, was Alexander's spiritual adviser throughout his campaign in India. Arrian (Greek historian) wrote that no history of Alexander would be complete without the story of the Naga Sadhu (Calanus).

Upon request from King Alexander, he accompanied the Greeks as they were retreating from India.

He was 73 years of age. He could not take the rough journey and the chilly weather. He was scared and worried about getting disabled. He was a devotee of Lord Shiva, and the journey upended his intense spiritual practice. He suffered intense fear of dying—a medical condition called "Thanatophobia," death anxiety. He decided not to continue the westward march with the Greek army. He wanted to end his life, with his own hands, by self-immolation.

He requested to meet King Alexander to tell him about his decision not to continue the journey. The king asked him what he wanted to do and how he would return to India. Surprised, the Sadhu replied that he would not go back to India and that to solve this conundrum, he would die with his own hands by self-immolation (setting fire to himself).

Alexander tried his best to dissuade him from his decision, but upon the insistence of Calanus, Alexander relented.

Alexander asked Ptolemy I, one of his most trusted companions and military officers, to build a funerary pyre.

Calanus, before self-immolating, splashed the pyre with clarified butter and aromatic herbs so that the king would not smell his burning flesh. The king and his entourage stood around the pyre and tried to dissuade him again from this horrific act, but to no success. Before walking into the burning fire, Calanus stood in front of Alexander. He looked into the king's eyes for a moment and said his last words: "We will meet in Babylon."

Alexander and his admirals were surprised and puzzled—they had no plans to travel to Babylon. Calanus would be dead after self-immolating, and why he was telling the king about meeting him in Babylon. Alexander's journey back from India proved to be the most ardous part of his India campaign. Instead of returning the way he came over the Hindu Kush mountains, he changed his travel plans and decided to go south by the sea and finally arrived in Babylon. Alexander journey back from India proved to be the most arduous part of his Indian campaign.

Instead of returning, the way he came to India over the Hindu Kush mountains, Alexander changed his travel plans and decided to go south by the sea and arrived in Babylon.

No one understood Calanus's words, "We will meet in Babylon." It was only after Alexander fell sick and died in Babylon on June 11, 323 BCE, at the age of 32, that the Greeks came to realize what Calanus intended to convey: he had predicted Alexander the Great's death.

Alexander first met the Naga Sadhu on the bank of the Indus River in India and learned about the Naga's philosophy of detachment from the material world. After listening to Calanus, Alexander realized that all his possessions were meaningless. He had conquered the world; almost the world had conquered him. After all his material achievements, Alexander realized the emptiness of the material world.

Alexander followed the philosophy of the Naga Sadhu. When Alexander died, he had three wishes. He said:

1. My physicians alone should carry my coffin.
2. I desire that when my coffin is transported to my grave, the path leading to the graveyard shall display the wealth I collected.
3. My third and last wish is that both my hands hang out of my coffin.

After his death, Alexander conveyed his Guru's message to the world.

The skilled doctors are powerless against the inevitable grip of death. All earthly riches remain firmly on earth, unable to accompany us to our graves. We enter this world with nothing and leave in the same way. Our most precious treasure is our time on earth.

Timeless wisdom teaches the importance of our finite time in the world. In the final analysis, time is the most precious commodity we have. We cannot hold time like gold or gems.

How we spend this finite time
will eventually define who we are.
Alexander's body was taken to Egypt.
It was transferred to Alexandria
and buried in a grand mausoleum.
—Prophecy of Naga Sadhu, Calanus

Like most people in the village, my father was a farmer cultivating a small piece of land. The soil of the farm was virgin, not violated by chemicals, and produced more than enough to feed the family.

My dad and his dad worked on the farm from morning till evening, and my mom, my grandma, and my sister stayed home, not allowed to work in the field. The division of labor was clear in my dad's house: the man's job was to provide food for the family.

In the afternoon, the family would have lunch in the field. Life was simple, wholesome, and uncomplicated. In the evening, my dad would come home and meet his neighbor, Salim Yousef. They were good friends, bonded by a love for Ghalib's ghazals and Rumi's poetry.

My mom desperately wanted a son so the family farm would stay within the family. To conceive a healthy son, she started a ritual of prayers and fasts. My sister was 10 years old, and Dad had been waiting for his son all these years.

She started praying to the goddess of fertility, Shashti, who bestowed children to the childless. Shashti worship is prescribed to occur on the sixth day of each lunar month of the Hindu calendar.

Finally, after 10 years of praying and fasting, Goddess Shashti blessed her with a healthy son—my brother. Dad celebrated this happy and watershed event in his life with sweets and gifts. As we know, there are no family secrets in a small village, so the whole village ended up celebrating my brother's entrance into this small, beautiful world.

The village was like a close-knit family. Hindus, Muslims, and Sikhs lived peacefully and worshiped their gods. There was social harmony, and unlike the national political and religious debate, the religious diversity in millions of small villages was not destroying people's lives.

Before my brother's second birthday, a tragedy hit the family. My mom woke up with the baby in her lap and was surprised to notice that he was quiet and not responding. She started singing a lullaby and rocking the baby. She whispered to my dad to wake up and asked, "Is he sick? What is wrong?" Dad took the baby near the window, desperately trying to get a response from a limp, unresponsive son. Once he noticed that the baby had turned blue, he rubbed the baby's stomach—no response—turned him over and slapped his back, but still no response. He started shouting, "Breathe, Raju, breathe!" but there was no response.

He looked at his wife and tilted his head upwards, as if looking at the heavens for an answer, and began crying. Mom knew that her precious little gift to Dad—my brother—was gone, and with this tragedy, the dreams of having a son to take care of the farm vanished like morning dew on a hot summer day.

She said to my dad, "All my years of prayers and fasts were wasted on the false goddess."

She stumbled out, crying and beating her chest. She went to the family temple and locked it, promising never to pray again. God was not an answer to her sufferings; with this tragedy, God became a big question, not an answer. Sometimes God is the most uninteresting answer to the most interesting questions.

After this life-shattering event, my mom changed. It broke her heart and drove her into deep depression—on the verge of insanity. She lost her faith and could not understand how a benevolent goddess could betray her.

She stopped doing daily prayer and stopped going to the temple for evening prayer. With her son gone, her goddess also vanished from her life. She would get up at night and wander around the house looking for her son.

Before this tragedy, Mom lived a simple life full of rituals and prayers. She would get up in the morning, warm water on the coal stove for my grandfather's bath, and then take him to the temple. Now she stopped all her rituals and refused to clean the small family temple.

She stopped listening to spiritual music and told my dad that God is an illusion, a mirage. People who follow a mirage will never find real water. A total metamorphosis from a devout Hindu to a hard-core atheist.

Our faith anchors us to our sanity, and with this tragedy, both Mom and Dad were lost. My dad also stopped going to the temple, and he would fight with his mom whenever she suggested that he should pray and do the daily rituals.

When Dad's friends learned about the tragedy, they decided to help in their own ways. They would come to the house in the evening and bring food to share with our family. Over time, Mom started coming out of her deep depression.

One evening, our neighbor, whom my sister called Uncle Yusuf, visited our house. He brought a box of sweets and told my mom and dad that his younger brother was blessed with a healthy son, and this miracle only happened after he prayed at the Dargah.

Uncle Yusuf, known for his helpful nature and mild manners with a gentle smile, requested that my mom and dad not give up on God. He said, "For us humans, giving up on God is never an option; accepting His will and moving forward is the only way to live a meaningful life."

He suggested that my parents follow the same ritual as his brother—go to the Dargah of a Sufi saint and ask for a son.

Uncle Yusuf had no hesitation in telling his Hindu friend to pray for a son at the shrine of a Muslim saint.

Pakistan, which is solely associated with Islam, is in fact the birthplace of several prominent religious movements. Scattered all over Pakistan are countless shrines of the Hindu, Buddhist, Jain, Sikh, and Islamic religions. Before the partition, India was divided by different princely states, which were ruled by Muslim as well as Hindu princes. There were no restrictions for pilgrims to travel through different states. Hindu pilgrims could travel through a Muslim princely state and vice versa.

This time-honored tradition of crisscrossing different states for pilgrimage kept fragmented India united at the core of its spirituality.

The Dargah: The tomb of a Muslim Sufi saint. India is home to many Dargahs. The Sufis were liberal among Muslims. They spread the message of love of God and love of all humanity (not Muslims only). While Sufis are Muslims, they believe that there are other ways of approaching God, not merely Islam. In India, Sufis can relate to Vedanta in their interpretation of the nature of God. Sufis believe that every community has its path for reaching God.

My Dad, being a Hindu, had no conflict of faiths. He had no hesitation in praying and asking the Sufi Muslim saint for a son. There was this beautiful symphony of polytheistic and monotheistic religions living side by side in millions of villages before the British poisoned the people with their toxic narrative and politics of "Divide and Rule."

Mom and Dad decided to visit the Dargah located about 400 miles from their village in the state of Rajasthan. Uncle Yusuf and his brother helped my dad with the travel arrangements and offered financial help, which my father refused with a brotherly hug.

The Dargah was famous for its wish-fulfilling power. It is believed that if you ask for a wish with a pure heart, the wish will be fulfilled. Uncle Yusuf told my mom, whom he used to address as *Bhabhi Ji* (the wife of his brother), that the Dargah was also visited by the Mughal Emperor, praying for a son.

My mom asked Uncle Yusuf, *Bhaiya* (Brother), "We are Hindus, and I am a woman. I heard that only Muslim men are allowed to pray at the Dargah?" She further said,

"I will only go to this Dargah if I am allowed to pray with my husband."

Uncle Yusuf assured her and said, "Seventy percent of visitors are Hindus, and there are no restrictions for women. Women are allowed to go up to the Saint's grave."

This piece of information convinced my mom, and she decided to accompany my dad on the pilgrimage. After a couple of days of suffering the heat and congestion of crowded trains and bus rides, they arrived safely.

The moment Dad saw the white marble dome of the shrine, he felt a strange vibration and shiver going through his body, as if God had accepted him at the shrine. He told my mom about the strange feelings and said, "Shanti, we are in the right place, and if we pray here without doubt and with full faith, God will listen to our prayer."

The shrine, as seen today, was built in 1523 in memory of a saint and philosopher. The dome is an example of Indo-Islamic architecture and features a lotus and a crown of gold. The saint was born in Sanjar (of modern-day Iran). From Iran, he moved to India. He became a compassionate spiritual preacher and teacher. He was unanimously regarded as a great saint.

My parents followed the rituals – they offered a white silk *Chaddar* (sacred sheet) and rose petals to the shrine. After completing the ritual, they had their photograph taken by a professional photographer who happened to be a Hindu.

This was a unique experience because they had never had their photograph taken before. My mom kept that photograph in the family temple for the rest of her life; for her, it was more than a piece of paper.

At the Dargah, the pilgrims are served free food called *Langar* (food from the Cauldrons). The Cauldrons were donated by Emperor Akbar.

The *Langar* food is vegetarian and consists of rice, ghee, cashews, almonds, and raisins.

The Dargah is a classic example of the integration of Hindu and Muslim traditions. Tansen was a Hindustani classical musician. He was born into a Hindu Gaur Brahmin family. The Sufi Dargah influenced his music. Emperor Akbar invited him to sing in his palace, and he finally became one of the *Navaratnam*, a group of nine extraordinary people in the emperor's court.

Sandalwood paste and *Ittar* used in the Dargah come from a Brahmin family. Sikhs revere one shrine in the Dargah complex.

They returned to the village safely and got back into their routine. Over time, sweet memories of the pilgrimage started fading, life resumed its slow pace, and Dad got busy taking care of the family.

One night, Dad woke up with the same strange feelings he had experienced while visiting the Dargah. He got up from his bed, went to the family temple, and started praying. Finally, when he fully recovered from this dream, he told his mom that Goddess Shashthi came in his dream and said she would soon bless him with a healthy son.

The Goddess also said that the boy will live a long life if he sincerely and faithfully fulfills the Goddess's demands.

My mom was surprised to hear about this strange dream. She asked my dad what the Goddess' demands were. She said, "I will do whatever the Goddess wants me to do." She further said that her life was not worth living if she could not give him a son to protect and take care of his cherished farm."

Dad says, "The Goddess wants us to call our son 'Beggar Boy,' and the first shirt that he would wear after his birth, we must beg for money, and with that money we have to buy cloth for his shirt. When our son is one year old, he should wear gold hoop earrings, and we should not cut his hair for two years."

My mom was happy to hear about these demands and told Dad that by making these simple demands, the Goddess was blessing and forgiving us for the loss of our faith in her.

Our faith has a fleeting quality. When faith and fear go hand in hand, then it is a false faith. True faith is like a lighthouse; it will be there during bad as well as good times.

"By true faith, Moses, when he was grown up, refused to be called the son of Pharaoh's daughter, choosing rather to be mistreated with the people of God than to enjoy the fleeting pleasures of sin. God is most glorified in us when we are most satisfied with Him."
— Hebrews 11:24–26

PART 2

"1945 - Beginning of a new Chapter."

One fine morning, Mom was getting ready to take Dad's father to the temple, and his mom came out to see that they had a bouquet of flowers for the goddess. She looked at my mom and smiled, and she pulled back Mom's head cover (out of respect, it was customary in our culture to cover the head while in the company of your father-in-law). She wanted to confirm her suspicion. She noticed discoloration on Mom's face. She rushed to the family temple and rang the temple bell. This was her way of thanking the goddess for her blessings.

She came out of the temple smiling and said, "Shanti, the goddess has blessed you with a child." Mom knew that her mother-in-law was right.

Mom rushed to Dad's room; she wanted to tell Dad the news herself before he heard from his mom. She was waiting for the right occasion to tell him. She found him in a deep sleep. She looked at his face—a face of a kind and hardworking man. The face of a man who made her complete. After the death of her child, she always felt that part of her was missing. She quietly lay next to him, took his hand, and put it on her stomach.

He woke up and found her staring at him with a beautiful smile. He looked at his hand resting and cupping her belly, as if unconsciously holding the growing son. They stayed lying next to each other. No words were exchanged, and time stood still, not rushing this auspicious moment. waste. The goddess has blessed us with a child."

I was born in August 1945, two years before the partition of India. There was no hospital or clinic in the village; all the babies were born in a house. The babies were delivered with the assistance of a Daae. Every village in India had an untrained person called Daae, who provided expert guidance that she had learned on the job to support the mother during delivery.

The Daae is equivalent to Doula (in Greek), but Doulas are trained to guide and support the mother during delivery. The Daae is well-respected and compensated depending on the sex of the baby. There is no fixed amount, but families do their best to please the Daae.

While the Daae is mothering the mother, the rest of the family, mostly ladies and children, wait anxiously outside the room. With the sound of the baby's first cry, the celebration starts.

The Daae tells my dad it is a healthy boy. He goes to Uncle Yusuf's house with a box of sweets to give him the good news.

My coming into this beautiful world won't be complete without the blessings of the Hijras. Hijra is a Persian word. It has been loosely translated into English as a eunuch or hermaphrodite, where the irregularity of male genitalia is central to the definition. However, in general, most Hijras have been born male.

A typical celebration by Hijras starts without planning or invitation. One fine morning, a group of Hijras shows up at the house. The head of the group holds the newborn in her arms while the group members sing and dance in their inimitable style. Most people in Punjab believe a Hijra's blessing will confer fertility, prosperity, and long life on the baby.

After the singing and dancing ceremony, the group leader will tell the family the group's demands. These typically include cash and jewelry. The family will negotiate, and after some give-and-take, the matter will be resolved. The celebration will end with another round of singing and dancing. It is considered inauspicious to disappoint Hijras, and the family does its best to meet their demands.

My dad was ecstatic. With his friends, he started the celebration with XXX rum that he had been saving for many years for this occasion.

With my birth, my mom's depression gradually improved. She started going back to the temple. The sudden infant death of her first son created a deep fear in her mind. The tragedy of her son dying was still lurking at the back of her mind. The crippling anxiety, not knowing what was waiting around the corner for her newborn son, changed her behavior. She would not leave me out of sight, constantly worried about my breathing. She stopped going to the farms, and she would not trust anybody to take care of me.

She was also upset about losing her faith in the goddess. She wanted to redeem herself, so she confessed her sin in her mind.

One morning, after praying, she asked Dad, "For the protection of our son, the goddess told you to do all rituals within two years?"

Dad said, "Yes."

She said, "My atonement for losing faith in the goddess will be to pray and watch over my son for two years. At night, while he is sleeping, I will not sleep and will watch him. I will pray to the goddess every night till the rituals are done."

This penance is my way to redemption. It will give me peace of mind. My penance will protect my son, and with the goddess's blessing, his breathing will not stop while he is sleeping.

My mom did not sleep at night for two years. She only slept during the daytime. Dad was worried that she would get sick. He tried to change her and said, "Mother goddess is not heartless; she will protect our son."

Finally, Dad gave up when he saw a unique resolve and commitment in her eyes.

NAMAKARANA

The ceremony of naming a newborn baby is traditionally known as *Namakarana*. It is the name-giving ceremony in Hinduism and a *samskara* (rite of passage) to name a baby.

This is one of the most important of the 16 Hindu rituals. Mom, Dad, and all family members participate in this ritual. The family priest starts the ritual by chanting mantras from the holy book. After consulting the Vedic astrology and making sure that my birth star is in the proper constellation, the priest concluded that the first alphabet of my name should be "B"; my name should begin with "B," and he selected my name—Bhikshu, Sanskrit meaning Beggar—surprisingly, that was also one of the goddess's demands.

My dad was happy with this ceremony, but my mom was not happy because my name is Beggar Boy. She was worried about my future. She strongly believed that a person's name influences their destiny.

The ancient Romans even left a rhyme for this concept: *nomen est omen*, or "the name is an omen."

This theory generally does not stand the test of time. Your name does not decide your future. Your destiny is in your hands, and a sincere commitment to your life goals.

There is no scientific proof of nominative determinism, but **scientism**—that is, systematically explaining every aspect of our life journey—sometimes robs us of the wonder of the metaphysical world.

For humans, science is not only a justifiable access to the truth. The beauty and wonders of metaphysical claims are equally important—essential to making life interesting and worth living.

I survived, and after two years, there was a big celebration. I had my head shaved at the ceremony, called **Mundan**. During the Mundan ceremony, after the special prayer by a priest, the barber is assigned the task of shaving the baby's head. The ceremony is done between 4 months and 3 years after birth.

The life of a Hindu is full of rituals from birth to death; collectively, these rituals are known as **Samskaras**, meaning *rites of purification*, and are believed to make the body pure and fit for worship. (*A boy's first haircut—Mundan—is one such Samskara and is considered an event of great auspiciousness.*)

After the ceremony, my dad invited his friends for a special meal. He served a vegetarian meal consisting of rice, ghee, cashews, almonds, raisins, and vegetable curry. The meal was the same as he had when he visited the Saint Chishti's dargah.

Dad says to his friend, “Yusuf, this meal is the only way I can visit Saint Chishti and thank the Saint for his blessings.”

Rumors

Life in our small town was peaceful. Mom and Dad were happy that I was growing up and healthy. Mom started sleeping at night, and family rituals resumed, and Mom and Dad became more religious.

In the evening, prayers in the town's temple and **mosques** were recited on loudspeakers. Most people in the town were Muslims, with a few scattered families of Hindus and Sikhs. There was no sign of religious conflict, and a unique kind of social harmony made the lives of our town peaceful and wholesome.

Unfortunately, our town and millions of small villages in India were living in bubbles. Due to a lack of media outlets, the people living in small villages were totally ignorant about national politics. The partition of India was the last thing on people's minds—a rumor not worth wasting time. How misinformed and wrong they were.

The religious differences in the Indian National Congress were tearing the country apart. Rumors circulated that the Hindu-dominated Indian Congress was on the verge of splitting into the Muslim League, under Mohammad Ali Jinnah, and the Indian National

Congress, under Mohandas Gandhi and Jawaharlal Nehru.

The British historian Patrick French, in *Liberty and Death*, shows how much this political fight between the leaders came down to a clash of personalities among the politicians of the period, particularly between Muhammad Ali Jinnah, the leader of the Muslim League, and Mohandas Gandhi and Jawaharlal Nehru, the two most prominent leaders of the Hindu-dominated Congress Party. All three men were anglicized lawyers who could have been close allies. But by the early 1940s, their relationship had grown so poisonous that they could barely be persuaded to sit in the same room.

Jinnah was undoubtedly a tough, determined negotiator and a chilly personality. He was a staunch secularist, drank whiskey, rarely went to mosque, and was clean-shaven and stylish. He chose to marry a non-Muslim woman, the glamorous daughter of a Parsi businessman. She was famous for her revealing sari and for once bringing her husband a ham sandwich on voting day. He was the architect of the Islamic Republic of Pakistan.

In 1946, Mr. Nehru told journalists there would be no communal trouble in India when the British left.

In August 1947, in the first address to the Constitutional Assembly of Pakistan, Jinnah said, "You may belong to any religion or caste or creed—that has nothing to do with the business of state." But it was too late; by the time the speech was delivered, violence between Hindus and Muslims had spiraled beyond anyone's control.

Jinnah's motivation to create the Islamic Republic of Pakistan was not ideological but personal. The British helped him. — He was backed by British imperialists, notably Churchill, who believed Pakistan would prove a faithful friend to the West and a buffer zone between communist Russia and socialist India.

Jinnah also helped the British achieve their geopolitical goal. He left behind wounds of division and hatred among the Muslims and Hindus. These wounds still have not healed.

This catastrophic event, the Partition of a prosperous, inclusive India, was caused by the British Empire.

By partitioning India, the British achieved their geopolitical goals of disharmony and segregation of communities - executed in terms of geography. The partition caused a religious fracture in the social fabric of the subcontinent and isolated both Hindus and Muslims.

During its colonial era, the British perfected and nationalized differences based on identity among its subjects.

FLIGHT

It is midnight; somebody is gently knocking at our door. Mom is scared, and she tells Dad not to open the door. She is worried because rumors about communal violence make her cautious. The gentle knocks on the door do not stop, and finally, Dad opens the door. He is surprised to see Uncle Yusuf and his brother standing on the veranda. Their faces are covered as if they are trying to protect their identities.

They come inside the house, and Dad closes the door. They tell Dad the bad news that will change his family's life forever.

Uncle Yusuf says, "Satish, take your family and leave the town as soon as possible. I met a few hard-core members of the Muslim League — the sectarian violence has already started between Hindus and Muslims. The last train coming to our town had dead bodies and many wounded passengers with the message: 'THE PRICE OF BETRAYING THE MOTHERLAND.' They are planning to start killing all Hindus to send a message back to India."

After listening to this bone-chilling news, Mom starts crying.

She asks Dad, "Where are we going to migrate? This is the only home we have known all our lives." Then she says, "The Goddess's prophecy — to name our son 'Beggar Boy' — will be fulfilled once we leave the farms. We'll all be living like beggars in this new India."

There was pin-drop silence, as if time stood still. There were so many questions but no answers. In the dimly lit room, with an oil lamp flickering in the gentle breeze, Dad looked at his family and saw his mom crying while his dad was holding her hand.

At that moment, Dad's dreams of giving the farm to his son vanished like morning dew on a hot summer day. He was staring at an abyss, not knowing what to do—should he listen to Yusuf's advice and leave his land, or should he stay put and hope for the best? He looked at his family, closed his eyes as if asking his God to show him the way—he opens his eyes and looks at the family again. There is pin-drop silence in the room, waiting for his decision. Finally, in a low-pitched voice, he says, "We are going to leave and hope for the best. If there is life, there is hope. There is no hope for the dead. Nobody controls our destiny except God—let's pray to God to give us strength so that we can carry **our cross** with our humanity intact."

Uncle Yusuf tells Dad that he has plans to get the family across the Jhelum River on the Indian side of the border. He and his brother's fishing boats are already anchored and ready to go. My mom and grandmom will wear burkas to hide their faces, and my dad and his dad will hide by lying down on the floor. My dad and his family will sail with Uncle Yusuf, and his brother will help Dad's mom and dad cross the river.

Dad, with tears in his eyes, says, "Yusuf, before we leave this beautiful land, I want to give you my farm—our most precious possession. This gift, nobody deserves it more than you."

We will never forget your kind act. If I survive this carnage, you will be in my prayers for the rest of my life."

Uncle Yusuf is surprised to hear Dad's gift offer but says nothing. Dad tells him to wait and goes to his bedroom.

Dad brings his farm and house ownership papers and offers them to Yusuf, saying, "Yusuf, when we are gone, I would like you to claim my land as yours."

This surprises Yusuf. He refuses to accept Dad's offer and says, "Satish, you take these papers with you. Once peace and sanity return to our people, you can come back and start your life afresh. This land belonged to your ancestors, and it should go to your son."

Dad insists and forces the ownership papers into Yusuf's hand. Uncle Yusuf gets annoyed. He angrily looks at Dad and then takes a matchbox from his pocket and says, "Satish, I would rather burn these papers in front of everybody than accept them."

This surprises Yusuf's brother, who tries to intervene, but Uncle Yusuf raises his hand, signaling to his brother to back off. There is a unique kind of resolve in his eyes, indicating that he will not accept Dad's offer.

By refusing to accept Dad's land papers, Uncle Yusuf made it crystal clear that he had no other motive but to protect and help his friend escape the oncoming apocalypse.

In his mind, Yusuf thought that if he accepted the land gift, people and his friends might think that he had ulterior motives and bad intentions—creating panic and scaring us into leaving so he could grab our land.

Uncle Yusuf's refusal, and even the act of burning the land papers, made it clear and validated his sincere intentions to help Dad save his family from the bloodbath.

Uncle Yusuf and Dad had been friends since childhood, and both families had been living in peace for generations. Their farms were next to each other. Uncle Yusuf, after hard work on the farm and before going home, would come to our house and have evening tea with hot vegetable fritters. He loved my mom's tea, a concoction of tea, cardamoms, and ginger, boiled with fresh milk—not a simple tea, but a symphony of all the spices in harmony.

Uncle Yusuf was a gentle giant—tall, muscular, with a thick neck. He had a pleasant and non-threatening demeanor. He had a square face with a strong chin and always kept a well-groomed head. He was a devout Muslim in his food habits but did not like to go to mosque on a regular basis. One time, Dad asked him, "Yusuf, how many times in a day do you pray to Allah?" His answer was, "Each breath comes out with Allah's name." He was a true Muslim: for him, his humanity and love for his friend were more critical than the man-made religion and its rituals.

During the partition of India, the bad news and horrific human behavior were overwhelming, but that was not the full picture of India's Partition. The bloodbath and murders of Hindus and Muslims overshadowed the acts of millions of Hindus and Muslims doing the right things. These God-fearing people did not sacrifice their humanity, kindness, and empathy for the sake of man-made religions.

Our tendency towards goodness has been a significant driver of our evolution as human beings. The human connection is our most defining characteristic. Friendship and love of fellow human beings are vital to us. Many decades ago, they found that at the base-pair level—the building blocks of DNA—all human beings are 99.9% identical. A lot of variation resides in that 0.1%, but the level of similarity is mind-boggling. Our shared desire for dignity transcends all our differences.

During India's partition, the sectarian violence behind the shield of religion lost its shared humanity. Religions have no value without humanity, which is the cornerstone of all religions. Religion, as a way of life and belief system, connects humanity with spirituality and often moral values.

Without humanity, religion is just a cheap show of man-made rituals.

The Migration

On the day of our migration, the Jhelum River was calm. After crossing the river and safely disembarking on the Indian side, Uncle Yusuf and Dad had a tearful hug and said *Inshallah* to Yusuf and his brother, the family set off to the nearest railway station on the Indian side of the newly demarcated border.

Crossing this border was the most transformative experience for my family. The border divided people who had similar ways of life and spoke the same language.

After the Partition in 1947, the emergence of the new nations of India and Pakistan was accompanied by 14.5 million people moving across newly defined borders. This was marked by large-scale communal violence and deaths.

On the platform, Dad finds the railway staff hosing down the blood. Dad changed his mind and decided to walk with the other refugees. The bloodshed and killings going on all over the land were horrific and sickening. During the Partition, mass movements attracted the most heinous crimes like killings, looting, abduction, and rape.

The two states, Punjab and Bengal, geographically became the focal points of inhuman brutality. The methods of violence were unimaginable—attacks on trains, deliberate derailments, and physical humiliations of innocent people.

During communal rioting, women and children were heavily targeted. Women and girls, always protected in the family cocoon, were worst caught in the dilemma—the open territory became an easy hunting ground for animals who were roaming around in the disguise of humans.

In the world of writer Hijari, "Pregnant women had their breasts cut off and babies hacked out of their bellies, infants were literally found roasted on spits." Violence played a significant role in explaining the mass exodus and migration.

My dad had the awesome responsibility of protecting the family. He joined the largest column of marching people of different families called *Kalifas*, meaning several households coming together to form a caravan.

My sister asks Dad, "Where are we going?"

Dad looks at my mom and says, "Wherever God takes us. Thank God we are alive and together as a family."

The caravan slogs along at a snail's pace, and it smells of wet clothes and babies crying. My sister stays at my dad's side, and my mom is carrying me to protect me from the sun; she covers my head with a wet towel.

My sister asks Dad, "How far is India? My feet hurt."

"We are in India," Dad says, and he picks her up.

"Is there food for us?"

"Yes."

"How much food do we have, Papa?"

"Are you hungry?"

"No, Papa, but we should save as much food as we can."

"Kamla, I will never let you starve, so whenever you feel hungry, let me know," Dad says.

Before night falls, Dad wants to reach the nearest village because he is worried about the safety of his family. God must be listening to his prayers—Dad faintly sees a flag fluttering in the gentle breeze. It is a triangular yellow/saffron flag made of cotton or silk with a tassel at the end that is hoisted on a tall flagpole. It serves as a beacon and announces the presence of a Gurdwara. The flag is called "Nishan Sahib." The symbol on the Nishan Sahib is the Khanda and is considered the emblem of the Sikh faith.

The Punjabi word "Gurdwara" literally means "the residence of the Guru" or "the door that leads to the Guru." A Gurdwara is a place of assembly and worship for Sikhs. The first Gurdwara was built by the first Guru, Guru Nanak Ji, in 1521–1522 in Kartarpur, on the bank of the Ravi River, which is presently situated in Pakistan.

Sikhism is a religion and philosophy that originated in the Punjab region of the Indian subcontinent around the end of the 15th century CE. It is one of the most recently formed major religious groups and stands as the fifth largest worldwide, with about 25–30 million adherents. Sikhism developed from the spiritual teachings of Guru Nanak Ji (1469–1539), the first Guru.

Guru Nanak Ji taught that living an active, creative, and practical life of truthfulness, fidelity, self-control, and purity of thoughts establishes union with God.

The Sikh scripture—Guru Granth Sahib—opens with a fundamental prayer about "Ik Onkar" (One God).

Dad says, "Kamla, a Gurdwara is coming our way." Dad sees a smile on Kamla's face because she knows that in the Gurdwara, there will be delicious Langar waiting for her. She suddenly jumped out of Dad's lap and started running towards the Gurdwara.

In Sikhism, a Langar is the community kitchen of a Gurdwara which serves meals to everyone free of charge, regardless of religion, caste, gender, economic status, or ethnicity.

The Langar was started by the first Guru, Sri Guru Nanak Dev Ji. Guru Sahib's father gave him money to start a business, but he met some sadhus and fed them with that money. The basic concept of Langar is to feed the needy, keeping with the philosophy of Sikhism—Seva (selfless service). The Langar kitchen is maintained and served by members of the Sikh community and volunteers.

The next day, with the help of the Gurdwara, our family safely got on the train heading towards a new India — a journey to a new life — a life of uncertainty and no destination. Dad had no friends or relatives living in this part of India. He was lost in his own thoughts, perhaps thinking not of what lay ahead of him, but of what he left behind — death and destruction. He was at peace knowing that his family was safe.

"Where are we going?" Mom says.

"We have no other option except to go as far as this journey takes us," Dad says.

At the last station, our family, along with fellow refugees, gathered on the platform and decided to walk to the town center, looking for shelter and food.

There was no agency to guide or help us. After the partition and migration of Muslim residents, this town became a purely Hindu town, with scattered mosques here and there. The Hindus living in this town had a different language (a Hindi dialect) and customs, and it felt as if we had come to a different country.

The family settled in Hissar, a town in the western part of Haryana state, India. Its southern and western portions mark a gradual transition to the desert, and the climate was entirely different from the Jhelum.

This area was a subtropical hot desert. The average maximum summer temperature hovers between 105°F and 110°F, and during summer, the hot air would burn the skin. The only saving grace was that the air had low humidity.

Our family was given a small house with a kitchen but no electricity. The house belonged to a Muslim family, because in one of the rooms, on a window sill, Dad found the family's holy book, *The Quran*, wrapped in silk cloth. Dad lifted the Quran, and there was a handwritten note saying, "Allah blessed you and your family with good health — take care of this house as yours. We have plenty of uncooked rice and beans in the kitchen."

Despite all the violence and bloodshed, the members of this family had not lost their humanity and compassion — a hallmark of a true human being. Dad picked up the Quran with the handwritten note and told Mom, "Save this. Who knows, one day I may meet my friend Yusuf, and I will give him this precious gift." And then Dad said, "I hope the family living in this house has safely migrated to Pakistan."

It is ironic that after giving Pakistan to Muslims, our family settled in the town of Hissar, whose founder was a Muslim Sultan, Feroz Shah Tughlaq. He named the city *Hissar-E-Firoza*, which means "Fort of Feroz." *Hissar* is also a Persian word meaning a *quilla* or a fort.

The Thin Crust of Civilization

During the Partition of India, the heinous crimes committed by so-called God-fearing civilized people unraveled the fundamental nature of any civilization.

The elementary staples of organized, civilized life are food, shelter, political power, and economic security. Once these staples are threatened, the civilized nature of humans, in a short period, goes back to a Hobbesian state. The civilization on which we tread, build monuments, and worship houses is always wafer-thin. Socio-economic unrest shatters the illusion of a rock-solid and stable civilization.

What happened during the Partition of India was horrible but not unique. History is full of such events. It happened during the Holocaust. The highly advanced German civilization crumbled overnight. Some of the world's greatest inventions originated in Germany, ranging from the mind-blowing theory of relativity to the humble aspirin. Home to Karl Marx and Albert Einstein, the contribution of German civilization in fields as varied as classical music to quantum physics is unmatched in the evolution of humanity.

The paper-thin crust between civilization and de-civilization can disintegrate both through external and internal turmoil. In a highly civilized and rich nation, a leader elected by the people can use diversionary hyper-nationalism to stay in power.

The stress from outside forces is less sinister, dangerous, and grave than the threat within. The overall strategy of dehumanizing people is more destructive to a civilized nation than an external threat from a hostile nation.

The central component of fascism is hyper-nationalism coupled with a strong leader. All civilizations have, from time to time, become a thin crust over the volcano of revolution, and nothing de-civilizes a nation more quickly and surely than a war.

The thin crust of civilization often features a cult of personality around an arrogant, deranged leader, the justification of violence, and the repeated denigration of the rule of law.

The German political landscape was dramatically affected by the 1929 Wall Street crash. The Great Depression brought the German economy to a halt and further polarized German politics. In 1932, the Nazis became the largest party in the Reichstag (German Parliament). Hitler's rise to power was completed in 1934 following the death of President Von Hindenburg. Hitler merged the Chancellery and Presidency and became the Führer, the sole leader of Germany—a classic example of a threatened economic staple cracking the thin crust of civilization. The byproduct of this de-civilization was countless miseries and the Holocaust.

> *"We were aware that Civilization was a thin and precarious crust erected by the personality and the will of a very few and only maintained by rules and convictions skillfully put across and guilefully preserved."*
> *—Society, by John Maynard Keynes, 1938.*

There is no nation on this earth that is immune to this fundamental nature of human civilization. Any nation's rock-solid civilization is an illusion—an organized instability. It is like a sandcastle that comes down with a whiff of strong wind.

"A New Beginning"

After losing our family farm and home in Pakistan, it was good luck that the family settled in the town of Hissar in the state of Haryana. A mid-size city known for its fertile agricultural land, the area is also famous for small family-owned dairy farms.

The town is located about 102 miles west of New Delhi, India's capital.

It has a continental climate with very hot summers and relatively cold winters. Its southern and western portions mark a gradual transition into the desert. Most of the population are followers of Hinduism—in a way, a blessing for the families that were victims of religious and sectarian violence. The area is famously known as the breadbasket of India. In the years to come, this city will house Asia's largest Agricultural University, a leader in agricultural research in India.

The Agricultural University contributed significantly to the Green and the White Revolutions in the 1960s–1970s.

The famines of British India became a distant memory. The Green Revolution made India self-sufficient in food. After achieving this milestone and the capacity to feed its bulging population, India was no longer hostage to the whims of Western power geopolitics—finally a free nation to act and safeguard its national interests.

Once our family found shelter, Dad started looking for a job to put food on the table. Mom quietly slips a gold coin into Dad's hand to get money to buy food for the family. Before leaving the house, Dad tells his dad not to go out and look for a job because he was worried that the stifling summer heat would hurt him.

Dad would leave in the morning and come back at night, dejected and depressed because of no luck in finding work. This went on for a couple of weeks, and finally, one evening, Dad came home with a smiling face. My mom knew right away that Dad got the job.

Dad tells us he has been hired as a helping hand. He will take care of a small dairy farm. He is carrying a small canister filled with milk.

He tells Mom, "Let's celebrate today with rice pudding." The tradition of serving rice pudding is deeply embedded in Hindu culture. It embodies prosperity and purity. For Dad, rice pudding symbolizes a celebration and the end of a painful journey.

When we were in Pakistan, Mom used to make rice pudding every week. After migrating to India, a simple dish of rice pudding ignited a spark of hope in Dad's shattered life. He was happy to get this new job that would enable him to feed his family.

During dinner time, Grandpa said, "Bhikshu, the rice pudding we are eating today is more than a sweet luxury.

It is a ritual; the ingredients used in making rice pudding are considered pure and holy in Hindu traditions."

Before eating, he tells Mom to take the rice pudding to our Goddess and have her bless our home and purify it.

For my grandpa, seeing his family eat the rice pudding after all the suffering and hardship was an auspicious and cathartic ritual.

TRAGEDY

Life resumed its slow pace. Dad was happy to start a new life in our own India. Finally, Dad was at peace with himself. He managed to save the family from the carnage of India's partition, and now, with his hard work, we had a roof over our heads and food on the table.

Finally, after a turbulent and rough time, Dad thought that he had created a stable life for us; however, stability, in any form, is an illusion. It is an illusion that we actively cultivate and desperately hold on to. Stability is just a sandcastle; the core foundation of the castle is organized instability. Evidence of this law of nature is everywhere: change is constant in the universe.

Despite repeated warnings, my grandpa would not stop looking for a job to supplement the family income. Finally, he came home to tell us that he would be taking care of a rich man's garden and lawn.

Before the partition of India, Grandpa was retired. He had handed over his farms to Dad. My mom would accompany him to the temple for morning prayer, and the rest of the day, he would spend reading Hindu scriptures and buying fresh vegetables and other provisions for the family's dinner. His retired life was wholesome and relevant.

Now with his new job, he gets up in the morning already tired and washed out from the previous day's hard work. He will not stop working, despite knowing that the summer heat is hurting him—like termites, eating away at his health.

One night, after dinner, my dad looked at Grandpa's tired face and said, "Pa, you have lost weight. Please stop working. This is not our Jhelum; Hissar town is on the edge of the desert. This brutal and unforgiving summer is hurting and destroying your health."

Grandpa says, "I cannot sit home and see you struggle to put food on the table." He looks at me and continues, "What kind of message and lesson will Bhikshu learn? I would rather die working than sit home and wait for death to knock at the door." He warns Dad that this is the last time he will have this kind of discussion, and if Dad insists, he will not join the family for dinner.

The fear of becoming irrelevant at this stage in his life compelled him to keep on working.

All his life, Grandpa never complained of headaches, and now, after mowing the lawn on a hot summer afternoon, he started complaining of headaches and muscle cramps. He was not able to sleep because of the cramps. Dad was worried that he would get sick, but he did not have the courage to tell him not to work.

One day, while mowing the lawn, Grandpa complained of dizziness and passed out right in the middle of the lawn. Nobody was around to help him, get him into the shade, or give him a sip of water.

The rich man and his family members were having a siesta in the house. The windows were covered with thick blinds made of bamboo mixed with aromatic herbs. To keep the house cool, water from poorly designed sprinklers dripped on the blinds.

My grandpa lay there in the scorching heat, and by the time a passerby noticed him, he was no longer in this world.

He died with his dignity intact. In a way, he prophesied his own mortality—a proud, hardworking landowner who was not ashamed of mowing the lawn in unforgiving summer heat to help his family. It was an unfair deal for my grandpa, but who says **life is fair** for everybody?

VIDYARAMBHAN

I am now five years old, the right age to join school. Dad requests our family priest to do the ritual of Vidyarambhan. As the name suggests, *Vidya* means knowledge, and *arambhan* means start. This ritual marks the formal introduction of kids to writing and the syllabary.

This ceremony is often held between the ages of 2 to 5 years. The ritual starts with a special prayer dedicated to the goddess Saraswati, the goddess of knowledge and wisdom. Dad asks me to sit in his lap and covers my head with a saffron-colored silk towel. Our priest is sitting opposite Dad, and in the middle, there is a tray filled with rice.

The ceremony begins. The priest writes with his finger on the rice, "Om Hari Sree Ganapathy Namaha." Dad holds my right index finger and guides it to write the same mantra, and then my name, Bhikshu.

Different **Vidyarambhan** rituals signify different objectives. For example, writing on sand signifies practice, and writing on rice symbolizes the acquisition of knowledge that leads to prosperity.

At the end of the ritual, Mom takes the blessed rice and mixes it with other rice, nuts, and raisins. She cooks rice pudding. She offers the first serving of pudding to our goddess, and then she serves the priest before serving the rest of the family members.

Before the British arrival, India had widespread primary school education. The schools were built on revenue-free land. To maximize revenue, the British confiscated most of the land from the schools, and by 1830, the small schools no longer stood as vital centers of learning.

At the most basic level, British colonial policy in India massively underfunded education. Public spending on human capital in British India was among the lowest in the world. In British India, spending on human capital was 3% of the budget.

In 1813, the British Parliament enacted an annual budget of 1,000 pounds to improve education in India. Twenty years later, the sum increased to 100,000 pounds.

My primary school is in our neighborhood, just a few blocks away from the house. The school is housed in a large hall that was partitioned into different sections. The school has no chairs or tables. We are asked to bring a small carpet to sit on and a writing slate with chalk. At the end of the school day, we fold our carpet and take it home. The front wall of the room has a large hanging blackboard. Our teacher has a limited supply of chalk. The school has no playground, no electricity, but a hand pump for drinking clean, fresh water.

Our school, unlike modern schools, lacked many things, but it had a loving teacher and a wholesome school environment. We never felt that we were going to a poor school. During lunch break, Mom would bring fresh, cooked hot food and milk to feed me and my sister. We would walk back home alone without worrying about being kidnapped.

My teacher's house was next to our school, and if the teacher was sick and did not show up to work, we students would go to his house, sit by his bed, and help him with mundane daily chores. It was our way of showing our respect and appreciation – *Guru Seva*, serving the teacher.

The concept of *Guru Seva* is deeply ingrained in Hinduism. *Guru* means teacher, and *Seva* is the concept of service to God. In Hinduism, the *Guru*, the teacher, is equivalent to God, and taking care of the *Guru* is considered a privilege. The teacher-student relationship is based on the genuineness of the teacher and the respect, commitment, devotion, and obedience of the student.

Our town was almost a pure Hindu town. The Hindu scriptures and mythologies were discussed and debated daily in homes and temples. According to the *Ramayana*, Lord Rama and his brother Laxman performed *Guru Seva* by pressing Guru Vishvamitra's feet and legs when he was sick. The blessing of the teacher is the most precious gift a student can ask for.

It was a different world that molded my childhood. My family could not afford to give me children's toys to play with, like bikes and bats. These material things were compensated by gifts that one could not buy with money.

My grandpa gave me the gift of cognitive stimulation by reading to me the stories from Hindu scriptures and mythologies. My dad gave us a home without domestic chaos. Our home did not have electricity or running water. Since we never had these comforts, we did not miss them. There was plenty of food, sprinkled with Mom's love. While growing up poor, I never saw my parents fighting or bickering over money.

Sometimes, when Dad had extra money, he would treat us by taking us to a Kulfi shop (Indian ice cream). We would sit at a nice table; I would sit on one side, my sister on the other side, and Dad in the middle, both of us holding his hands. Mom and Grandma would sit opposite us. Generally, Dad stays in a jovial mood at the Kulfi shop, but today, after sitting down, he was surprisingly quiet and in a pensive mood.

Mom asked Dad, "What is wrong?" Looking at him, she knew that something was bothering him.

Dad looks at Mom and Grandma and says, "I miss my friend Yusuf. When we were kids, we used to go together to eat Kulfi. I am worried about him."

Mom asks, "Why, did you hear any bad news from Jhelum?"

Dad says, "Lots of people in Jhelum knew about my friendship with Yusuf; he was like a brother to me. It won't be difficult for the hard-core Muslims to figure out that he helped us to escape the bloodbath and massacre.

Even Islam affirms God to be compassionate, merciful, and just. For these hard-core Muslims, we were infidels, and helping infidels is insulting Islam. According to their interpretation of the Quran, it is the sacred duty of a true Muslim—and his obligation—to kill infidels, not to help them.

This was not Yusuf's interpretation of the Quran. That is why he would seldom go to the mosque on Friday."

Dad was worried about Yusuf and his family's safety.

He was hoping that the Yusuf family might have migrated to India like many other Muslims. India's famous Bollywood singer Mohammad Rafi had a hair-cutting salon in Lahore, Pakistan. So, during Partition, he migrated to Bombay.

Mom looks at Dad, sees tears rolling down his cheeks, indicating deep-buried pain and quiet sufferings.

Yusuf's friendship with my dad was a sacred institution, and not having Yusuf's friendship in his life left a deep scar on his soul.

Now, Dad was a changed man; Yusuf's friendship was replaced with blessed loneliness. In Hissar, he was finding it hard to nurture the deep-seated friendship he had with Yusuf.

My school gave me a secure abode and a loving teacher to learn and evolve as a well-balanced kid.

A person's conduct as an adult is formed by their childhood environment. It is necessary that a child finds a healthy environment at home and in other places.

There is a profound meaning in the seventh line of the poem "The Rainbow" by William Wordsworth. In this line, "The Child is father of the Man." The man is the product of his habits and behavior developed in childhood.

Adverse childhood experiences have an everlasting toxic effect on the development of a child.

Money cannot buy the things that matter in our lives, whether as a child or as an adult.

In 1952, India won the gold medal in Field Hockey at the XV Olympics held in Helsinki (Finland). Field Hockey has a special place in the hearts and minds of Indians. Our school celebrated the event by giving us kids sweets. After the celebration, the school gave us a holiday.

I was fascinated by this proud moment in the history of our country. As I look back on my life, this was a watershed event. India winning a gold medal acted like an ignition—something outside touching something deep inside. I decided to become a Hockey player and wanted to win an Olympic medal. As it is said, children's imagination knows no bounds. It allows them to create their own version of the world and sometimes their destiny. Children are not yet fully socialized into the norms and expectations of society. They feel free to explore their imagination and creativity. This ignition moment touched some unknown parts of my consciousness.

A humble, inexpensive Hockey stick became a magic wand, and it helped me to overcome my poor childhood. It gave me priceless pleasure to show my skills at the playground. The sport of Field Hockey changed my destiny.

When Dad comes home, I run to him all excited and say, "Dad, buy me a Hockey stick. I want to play the game and go to the Olympics."

Dad is surprised to see me all charged up and animated. He says, "Bhikshu, I don't have enough money to buy you a Hockey Stick," and then he looks at Mom.

Mom looks at me and sees a disappointed kid whose dream of becoming an Olympic hockey player is evaporating like morning dew in the heat of poverty. Being a mother, it was hard for her to see me in this miserable situation.

She tells Dad, "I have a few Rupees. We can buy Bhikshu a used Hockey Stick. It will be cheaper than a new one." Without telling me, Dad buys a used hockey stick and a ball. The next day, Dad surprises me with this unique and precious gift—the happiest day of my life.

Our town had two beautiful public playgrounds, one for Field Hockey and the other for Cricket. Our school hired a new teacher who also became our coach to teach us the game. After school, in the evening, Mom would walk with me to the field, and I would practice. This was the beginning of my journey as a hockey player.

I loved the game. I had a pregame ritual and believed that it would improve my performance. Before the game, especially on the day of a match, I would go with my grandma to our temple and ask our priest to bless my Hockey stick. The Priest would touch the statue of our

Goddess' feet, and then he would touch my hockey stick. Most of the time, our Goddess did not disappoint me.

I felt like I did not find the game of Field Hockey; rather, the game found me. While growing up and evolving, I would think about how to improve my game and become a player worthy of going to the Olympics. It became a front-burner mission of my life. I was selected to play for my school, and finally, in my senior year, I became the captain of my school hockey team.

After I graduated from school, Dad wanted me to join him because his dairy farm business was booming, and he was thinking of expanding it.

I say to Dad, "I would like to join the college and continue my studies. You don't have to worry about the expenses because I am entitled to a hockey scholarship. If I maintain my grades, the college will cover my tuition and books."

In college, I paid more attention to Field Hockey, and at the end of the first semester, my grades dropped. It threatened the scholarship and my education. I hated the idea of working with Dad, and going back to taking care of cows was like going to prison. I wanted to spread my wings and change the direction of my predetermined destiny.

My mom's brother, who was a mathematics professor at the college, told her about my low grades.

When I came home after playing the game, Mom looked angry and, with a determined demeanor, confronted me and said, "Bhikshu, my brother told me about your grades." She continued, "How are you going to support yourself and make a living when you are grown up? There are no professional leagues to play for. How are you going to put food on the table for your family? And what would happen if you got hurt and were not able to play? You'd better pay attention to your studies. This scholarship is God's gift to you; cherish it and don't let it go to waste."

Mom's direct and common-sense advice hits me like a bolt of lightning. Her words of wisdom sink to the bottom of my consciousness.

In my high school, every year, we kids were given medical checkups and needed vaccinations. Our visiting doctor was the kindest person. He would come to our school dressed in a white shirt and white pants. He treated us like we were God's precious gifts to mankind.

Sometimes, our life journey changes with personal observations. When he was four, Einstein noticed invisible forces in the universe controlling the needle of the compass he held in his hand—an invisible force that became his life's work.

I idealized my school doctor and wanted to follow in his footsteps. I decided to change my major to premedical courses to become a physician.

Even though I was not able to become an Olympian, the sport of field hockey laid the foundation of my character. Being a team player requires a disciplined life with integrity and perseverance. I learned the art of giving and receiving so our team could win the game. Winning the game was more important than the personal fame of scoring a goal.

These values are sometimes overlooked and forgotten. However, these human qualities are important not only in sports but in life. Sports help us grow into well-rounded, balanced human beings. Sports have the power to heal and change our world. The transformative impact is way beyond the game.

This sea change in my thinking about my future was due to the love and wisdom of my simple, uneducated mother and the kindness of my schoolteacher.

Riots

Dad's dairy farm was prospering, and he started expanding his business. Since our town was famous for dairy cows and agricultural products, merchants from different parts of the country frequently visited the town. Dad started doing business with another dairy farm in the city of Bombay. He would buy the cows in Hissar and then take them to Bombay via a special freight train. We would be anxiously waiting for his return home because he would bring us fancy clothes from Bombay.

One time, after returning from his business trip, Dad tells Mom, "Shanti, next year I am planning to build a new home with running water and electricity. Our kids can stay home and study instead of going to the library. Bombay's merchants love my cows and want me to double the supply." He continues, "I have already bought the land next to our dairy farm for the house." Dad is happy and wants to celebrate these watershed events in his life. He takes us to a Kulfi (ice cream) shop where we all celebrate.

Dad's business model was very simple: he would buy cows from the farmers and reimburse them after selling them. All transactions were word of mouth. The business was built on trust, and Dad had a good reputation.

Finally, Mom and Dad started talking about saving money for my sister's dowry, and they were happy about their kids' future, but nobody knew about the future. We don't know what is waiting around the corner, and dreaming about a stable and predictable future is an illusion.

The predictability and stability in our lives are really organized instability — it does not take much to unravel, so to speak, a rock-solid stability.

By the time I was finishing my premedical education, Dad's business suffered a tremendous blow. The business he built with hard work came crashing down on him like a volcano; it incinerated the family's happiness. He sees the smoldering ashes covering his dreams for his family.

The partition of India on religious grounds left deep scars of resentment on the heart and psyche of Hindus as well as Muslims. India would see many religious riots over minor provocations between Hindus and Muslims, with countless deaths and miseries. Even after many years of partition, the legacy of the British policy of divide and rule is still creating riots and bloodshed in both countries.

Dad was in the city when sectarian riots between Hindus and Muslims started in Bombay over an incident that destroyed Dad's business: a Hindu priest was bringing his cows to the temple grounds, and on his way, he crossed in front of the mosque where Muslims were celebrating their religious event. The Muslims felt that the Hindus had planned this to disturb their celebration. This would escalate from verbal assaults to large-scale riots.

The dairy farm where Dad was selling his cows was owned by Muslims. It was set on fire, and with it, Dad's dreams also went up in smoke.

Dad came home from Bombay a defeated and broken man. He had a scruffy beard and sunken eyes. His clothes smelled as if he had not changed them for ages, and he had lost almost half of his weight. His hands were covered with dirty pieces of cloth.

Mom looks at him in shock and asks, "What happened?" — knowing well, whatever happened was not good for the family.

Dad says, "We lost everything. The business I built went up in smoke. God has not done with me yet," and then he looks at Mom and says, "How much more suffering must our family go through? We left Pakistan, but Pakistan has not left us." He tells Mom about the riots and how, in the effort to save his cows from the fire, he burned his hands.

After finishing the practice game, I came home and saw a large brown envelope half hanging out of the mailbox. I was waiting for the results of my interview to join medical school. I opened it with shaking hands, and to my utter surprise, I found out that I had been accepted to join the medical school — one of the best in the state of Punjab.

I ran into the house, all excited and charged up, to give this good news to my mom and make her proud.

I was surprised to see Mom sitting next to Dad in a somber mood. She was holding Dad's bandaged hands, and I saw Dad crying, tears dripping from his eyes — a terrible sight. I had never seen Dad crying before. Mom was wiping them gently with her hands and looking at Dad. I saw no hint of resentment or blame, but kindness, compassion, and love in Mom's eyes.

I ask, "Dad, what happened?"

Dad is too badly traumatized to speak; he beckons to Mom with his teary eyes. Mom tells me about Dad's misfortunes and how he got hurt.

After telling me about the misfortunes, Mom looks up and asks about the letter I am holding in my hand. I hesitate to tell them the good news — Mom asks me again about the letter.

I say, "Dad, I got accepted into medical school on a Hockey scholarship," and to ease his mind, I tell him that the scholarship will pay for my tuition and books.

Dad asks, "What about the rest of the expenses like boarding and food?" I say, "The rest of the living expenses the scholarship will not cover — we have to pay."

Dad looks at Mom and, in a broken and sad whisper, says, "Bhikshu, I'm sorry to tell you that I won't be able to send you the money. I borrowed heavily to expand the business, and now I'm penniless. Both my hands are burned, and God knows how long it will take me to get back to work."

Mom looks at me. There is pin-drop silence. The air in the room is thick and still, as if the miseries created by misfortune and poverty are holding it — time-interrupted, a predestined journey. For a long time, nobody says a word.

Finally, Mom says, "Bhikshu, we will not let you miss this wonderful opportunity to become a doctor and take care of God's children. I will make sure that you get the money, but you must promise me something in return."

I look at her and see a rock-solid determination in her eyes. It is said that our eyes are a window to our soul, and looking into her eyes, I saw a kind, caring mom who had decided to let her dreams go — take a back seat — so that her son could become a doctor.

I say, "Mom, what do I have to do to keep my promise?"

She says, "Bhikshu, you promise me that the money we send you will be used for your food and other basic needs. You will meet lots of kids from rich families, and these kids will have different lifestyles. They may be drinking and smoking. I don't want you to ape their way of life."

I say, "Mom, I will keep my promise. For me, it is more than a promise — it will become my covenant with you, and I will never drink alcohol or smoke while in medical school."

Dad looks at Mom with a surprised and confused demeanor and asks, "Shanti, how are you going to support his education?"

Mom says, "I will send him money by selling my jewelry." Mom never told Dad the secret of the gold coins. On the day of my graduation from medical school, my mom told us about her well-kept secret.

The Secret of Gold Coins

After Mom's marriage ceremony, just before her departure from her parents' home, Mom's dad takes her to his bedroom and gives her a gift: a heavy-set silk saree. He tells her, "This is a special gift, and you must promise me that you will only use it to protect and help your children in case something happens to your husband. Nobody should know about it until the time of its use."

Mom asks her dad, "You have already given me sarees—why one more saree?" Her dad replies, "This one is special. Look at its size."

She is surprised to learn about the nature of her special gift. The borders of this heavy-set saree had numerous hidden pockets, and each contained a large pure gold coin. The gold coins were hidden in such a way that one could only find them by lifting the saree.

Mom never discussed or told us about this special wedding gift from her dad. At the time of Partition, she managed to bring it to India. Every month, Mom would take out one gold coin, and with the help of her brother, she would send the money so I could fulfill my dream of becoming a doctor.

She was my Mother Goddess, who happened to be my mom. She was a true embodiment of motherhood. She was our family lighthouse and guided us during rough times. She had all the qualities of a Mother Goddess. God blessed her with feminine kindness and compassion, coupled with the *Shakti* (power) of Goddess Durga.

If my life is a book, my mother is my favorite chapter.

Doctor Bhikshu

The medical school I attended was in the holy city of Amritsar in the Punjab State in Northern India. The city lies about 15 miles east of the border with Pakistan. The city is home to the Golden Temple, one of the Sikh religion's most spiritually significant and most visited gurdwaras.

In Hindu mythology, the city of Amritsar is believed to be the ashram site of Maharishi Valmiki, the writer of the *Ramayana*. According to the *Ramayana*, Sita gave birth to Lav and Kush, sons of Rama, at the Ram Tirth ashram of Maharishi Valmiki.

Medical school was a lot of fun. Our medical school had a swimming pool, tennis courts, and a field hockey playground. We lived in a hostel—a form of low-cost, short-term shared social lodging where a student rented a bed. Four students shared a room. There were many hostels, and each hostel had its own cafeteria, which we called the "Mess Hall," where we would meet for lunch and dinner.

During my five years of medical education, I developed a special kind of bond and camaraderie that would stay with me for the rest of my life. My roommates became my extended family. Mom kept her promise. I graduated with good grades and started my internship at the university hospital affiliated with the medical school.

After our orientation and introduction, I started an internship in medicine. At the beginning of the internship, my life became miserable. The senior house physicians would make fun of my name.

They would ask, "Bhikshu, how can a doctor be a beggar? What kind of name would parents give to their son?"

I would respond with a smile, without answering their taunts. My name was becoming a gag name—a source of humor among senior doctors and nurses.

One day, after we took our morning round, while we were sitting with the nurses, my senior doctor asked me the same stupid question: How could a beggar be a doctor? He continued making fun of my name. I surprised him by answering, "A good physician is a beggar all his life."

These words fell on him like a heavy brick. The two nurses, in cahoots with him while he was making fun of my name, also stopped giggling.

Suddenly, there was a pin-drop silence in the room. He asked, "How can a physician be a beggar?"

I said, "We physicians should be praying and begging God to heal our patients."

He said, "Bhikshu, we doctors cure the patients with our medical knowledge."

I said, "Our treatment may cure the patient, but it is with God's blessings that he will heal. The healing power is in God's hands, and there is a big difference between curing someone and healing someone."

I told him the story behind my name, and how it was not my parents, but our goddess who picked my name, and how my mom finally had me after years of fasting and prayers.

After listening to my life story, the smirk on his face was replaced with a reflective and pensive demeanor. This conversation changed him, and he became my good friend and my mentor.

One morning, I was assigned to take care of a new patient who was transferred to our hospital from a small village. He was admitted with pneumonia complicated by severe respiratory distress and nutritional anemia.

When I entered the cubicle to examine the patient, I found that he was an emaciated young man with skin and bones. He had a round face, sunken cheeks, and unkempt long curly hair falling on his face, indicating malnutrition. He was hooked to an oxygen cylinder with a nasal cannula. He looked at me and, despite his suffering, still managed to give me a gentle smile.

His wife was sitting on one side of his bed. In her lap, her two daughters were sitting on each side. Her eyes were swollen and red from crying. Her face showed signs of suffering, accompanied by an uncertain future staring into the abyss, not knowing what else was waiting for her family. I felt the air in the cubicle and around this family saturated with deep, soul-crushing pain and sadness.

She looked at me and covered her head with a *chunni* (a long, shawl-like scarf), her way of showing respect for the doctor.

She asked, "Doctor Sahib, is my husband going to get well?" I looked at her and said, "We will do our best to get him well"—a vague and not very comforting answer.

She covered her face with the *chunni* and started crying, tears falling down her face. The little girls sitting in her lap started wiping her tears with the *chunni*. She kissed both girls and hugged them. This kind act by two little angels brought a smile to their mother's face.

She looked at me and said, "I have no living siblings, and our future depends on my husband."

I understand her predicament because, without the protection of her husband, she will have a hard time raising her daughters. She will be subject to all kinds of sexual and nonsexual harassment. There is no safe place for a young mother with two daughters.

Her husband shows no signs of improvement. Every day, there is worsening of bilateral pneumonia to a point that his lungs, even with maximum oxygen through a nasal cannula, are not able to supply oxygen to the rest of the body. Finally, he is put on a respirator and started on more potent but toxic antibiotics. These new antibiotics are not available in the hospital's pharmacy. Every morning, she will go to the private pharmacy and buy the medications, and before handing them to the nurses, she will close her eyes as if praying to God to help her husband.

Despite all our best efforts, there is no change in her husband's medical condition. Finally, he goes into septic shock with renal shutdown, and in the early morning, he has cardiac arrest and dies. Since I was the junior resident taking care of him, the senior resident assigns me the emotionally draining and most depressing job of letting the wife know that her husband passed away.

When I met her to give her this horrible news, she was sitting in the corridor, and her daughters were sleeping in her lap. She looks at me, and my demeanor tells her that things are not going well. When I give her the bad news about her husband, she puts her hands to cover her eyes, and I see tears rolling down her cheeks. She cries silently, her daughters sleeping peacefully—a hopeless and dangerous situation—a young mother with two daughters. Only God knows what they will go through in the coming years and what kind of hardship she will face raising two daughters on her own in our patriarchal and misogynist society.

I sit next to her, waiting for her to recover from this shocking news. She looks at me with teary eyes and says, "How am I going to take my husband's body back to our village?"

I say, "The hospital can make arrangements for the transportation." She says, "I have no money to pay for the transportation. I have spent all the money to buy food and sold my gold jewelry to buy the drugs to save my husband."

When she said, "I sold my gold jewelry, which Dad gave to me at the time of the wedding," I remembered how my mom sold her jewelry to educate me. I saw the same monstrosity—the dehumanizing poverty showing its ugly face in a different disguise.

This kind of bone-crushing poverty was everywhere in my hospital. Most of my patients were referred from small villages in horrible medical conditions. The lack of health care transformed minor ailments into catastrophic, life-threatening emergencies. As an adult, I realized the importance of money to take care of our basic needs and protect our self-respect.

Money is like air: when it is present, nobody notices it, but when it is absent, it is all anybody can think of.

In Asian countries, poverty is defined by a lack of money, but in the rich Western nations where the basic human needs are met by progressive social infrastructure, the definition of poverty changes—the profound deprivation brought on by unaffordable housing and homelessness, increased homicides, and alcohol and drug addiction.

In our modern and materialistic society, the worst thing that happened to poor people was not only a lack of resources but also our preconceived biases of labeling them as criminals.

A new study by the Columbia University research group has shown that the relationship between poverty and crime is far from predictable or consistent.

In New York City, Asians' relatively high poverty rate is accompanied by exceptionally low crime rates.

In the late nineteenth century, the impoverished Jewish, Polish, and German immigrants had relatively low crime rates, while Italian, Mexican, and Irish immigrants committed violent crimes at higher rates. During the Great Depression, violent crimes declined.

It is our culture that defines us, not poverty or a lack of resources. Our cultural identity and shared customs and beliefs shape our worldviews and how we interact with others. In some cultures, the concept of fate is deeply ingrained, and poor people don't blame rich people for their sufferings. The concept of "Fate" tenderizes our behavior and creates social harmony among different groups—the rich and the poor.

Working with poor patients and listening to their sufferings taught me a lifelong lesson: suffering teaches us compassion. When you suffer, as my family has, you can sympathize with someone's sufferings.

Suffering teaches us humility. A person who has lived a frictionless life will find compassion and mercy looking like a sinner.

"If you had not suffered as you have, there would be no depth to you as a human being, no humility, no compassion. Out of sufferings have emerged the strongest souls; the most massive structures are seared with scars."
— Eckhart Tolle

IMMIGRATION

"Trust yourself, create the kind of life you will be happy with. Make the most of yourself by fanning the tiny sparks of possibility into the flame of achievement."
— Foster C. McClellan

I graduated from medical school with good grades. I wanted to get into postgraduate courses to become a medical specialist. After graduation, I had no more financial means to continue my studies—funds from the Hockey scholarship had run out, and my mom had sold all her gold coins. While I was finishing medical school, Dad sold his house and dairy farm to pay off his debts.

Despite a mountain of impediments staring me in the face, I still had this deep-burning desire to become a medical specialist. After graduation, figuring out how to move forward and do post-graduation with limited resources was the most stressful time in my life.

As the Upanishads (Hindu Scripture) say:

"You are what your deep driving desire is,
As is your deep driving desire, so is your will,
As is your will, so is your deed,
As are your deeds, so is your destiny."

I did not know whether my destiny would change or not, but I just had to find ways to accomplish my goal. I was not ready to give up. At the core of my consciousness, I always believed that if my commitment and intentions to achieve my goal were sincere, God would guide me and show me the path to follow.

Sometimes our circumstances force us to make tough decisions. These decisions will have consequences that can make or destroy your deeply cherished dreams. Thinking about my future after graduation was like looking into an abyss and not knowing what hidden monsters were waiting for me at the other end. I had no other option but to walk through the smoke and see what lies on the side of the mountain—not moving forward was not an option.

The only way I could do my post-graduation and become a medical specialist was to leave India and immigrate to a country where I could support myself while doing the post-graduation.

Following the Second World War and the breakup of the British Empire, Indian migration to the UK increased through the 1950s and 1960s. During the same period, medical staff from India were recruited for the newly formed National Health Service. The Indian doctors were targeted as the British had established medical schools in India that conformed to the British standard of medical training.

My medical school was in the holy city of Amritsar, Punjab. It was established in the 1920s. In the beginning, the medical school was named after His Excellency, Sir

Bernard James Glancy, the Governor of the state, and called Glancy Medical College. The main teaching hospital affiliated with the medical college was Victoria Jubilee Hospital—named in commemoration of the jubilee celebration of H.E. Queen Victoria's rule.

The core curriculum of our medical college was similar to the medical core curriculum of British medical schools. This means that students who graduated from my medical college were allowed to work and do post-graduation in the UK.

After my interview at the British Embassy, I was selected to do an Externship (a one-month rotation to evaluate your language skills before starting the House Job) at Hackney Hospital, London, UK.

My decision to leave India would have far-reaching consequences in my life, and I hoped that once I started working in the UK, the sword of poverty hanging over my head would come down. I started seeing glimmers of light indicating the end of a dark and painful journey and, hopefully, the end of poverty.

After the overnight flight from New Delhi, I arrived in London with a carry-on bag. The money I saved while working in India was barely enough to buy me a one-way ticket to London. I entered the Hackney Hospital's administration office with the acceptance letter for the Externship. Mrs. Wolf, a slightly heavy-set lady, greets me with a pleasant smile and takes the letter.

After cross-checking my credentials, she says, "Dr. Bhikshu, welcome to Hackney Hospital." I say, "Thanks." She says, "Your Externship will start in two weeks." "Ok."

She surprised me when she said, “Please give me your mailing address and telephone number in London, and if there is a change in your schedule, I will inform you.”

I say, “Mrs. Wolf, I don’t know anybody in England. I am coming here directly from the airport.” She looks at me and then at her assistant and says, “Doctor, you can check in at the nearby hotel and let me know the hotel’s telephone number so I can reach you if there is a change in your schedule.”

I say, “Mrs. Wolf, after paying for the taxi, I have only a few dollars in my pocket. I was under the impression that the hospital would have accommodation for me.” She says, “The hospital will provide you with accommodation after four weeks of Externship.”

Mrs. Wolf looks at me, then looks out the window; it is snowing outside, and she looks at me again. My demeanor must have softened her, and a deep-seated motherly instinct kicks in Mrs. Wolf’s heart.

She looks at her watch and surprises me by asking whether I have eaten or not. I say, “I did not have the time to think about food.”

Mrs. Wolf arranged food and a room for me in the nurses’ hostel, and from that day onwards, she became my best friend and helped me with the paperwork to start my internship. “God works in mysterious ways.”

Life in London

Hackney is a district in East London, England, forming around two-thirds of the modern London Borough of Hackney. It is famous for its street art, which can be found all over the area. Hackney is also known for its thriving music scene and has produced several famous musicians and artists.

The hospital is in the borough of Hackney. It serves as a teaching hospital for students at Barts and the London School of Medicine and Dentistry, and provides postgraduate training in all major specialties. It was good luck that I was selected to do an internship in Hackney. I was not aware of this before joining the hospital.

Life in Hackney Hospital was full of surprises. We junior doctors were housed in a dormitory with single rooms and shared bathrooms. Our dormitory had a long, curvy corridor leading to a small bar and dining hall. The bar served beer but no hard liquor. The beer was dirt cheap because it was subsidized by Her Majesty the Queen.

Before coming to London, while in India, I never drank alcohol. Thanks to my friend Andrew Pembroke, I developed a taste for British lager in the hospital bar.

Because of the cheap beer, the bar was the most visited room in our dormitory.

In our bar, I met Andrew, the registrar in the Department of Medicine, where I was doing the internship. He was the nicest person I met while in London. He was tall, with deep, thoughtful blue eyes and straight blond crew-cut hair. He was extremely reserved, self-controlled, a classic example of the "stiff upper lip" with most of the junior doctors. While making rounds in the hospital, his bedside manners were impeccable. His room was next to mine in the dormitory, and sometimes he would invite me to his room to ask if I needed any help. I was fascinated by his mannerisms and his daily routine. Before going to bed, he would iron his clothes and polish his shoes. He believed it was an insult to his sick patients if he showed up shabbily dressed to care for them. He never left the hospital without carrying an umbrella, whether it was raining or sunny.

My first assignment as an intern was in the emergency room. Even though the British had been in India for centuries, and my medical education was in English, British culture was alien to me. The emergency rotation was an eye-opener. In the emergency room, I saw all kinds of patients and the cultural kaleidoscope of British society.

One fine evening, we were working in the emergency room, taking care of minor illnesses. It was a relatively quiet evening. The head nurse, Brenda McCay, was planning to treat us with her homemade cookies and tea. Brenda was the most beautiful Irish nurse, with blond bob-cut hair and a pleasant demeanor, I met while working in the hospital. Whenever Brenda was on call, most of the English doctors were hovering around and finding excuses to visit the emergency room to warm up their eyes with Brenda's smile.

Brenda was a few years older than I. She had a soft corner for me because, after finishing her rotation and before going home, she would invite me to the cafeteria for tea and a small apple pie. Brenda was married and had a son. Our friendship stayed platonic and was never corrupted by the toxic impulses of infidelity.

The quietness in the emergency room is an illusion, just like a deceptively calm-looking volcano rumbling at its core before eruption. In the middle of our tea break, we got an urgent call: the ambulance was bringing a middle-aged patient with unstable blood pressure and an evolving stroke. Brenda assigned the patient to me.

I entered the examination room and found a well-built, tall, middle-aged white man with a ruddy complexion. His face was distorted, and he was extremely restless and complaining of an excruciating frontal headache. He was not able to give me the history of his illness. His wife was standing next to him. She was well-dressed, with bobbed natural-colored hair, and her lips were shining with deep red lipstick. She must have taken a good amount of time before calling the ambulance for help to get into her sartorial splendor. The urgency of her husband's life-threatening medical condition must not have been a front-burning issue for her. She repeatedly looked at her watch, giving me the impression that she was anxious to leave this place.

Since her husband is unable to tell me about his complaints, I introduce myself and ask her, “Ma’am, how long has he been sick?” She says, “This morning when he woke up to go to the bathroom, I heard a loud thump and found him lying on the floor.” “Was he conscious?” I ask. “He was confused, complaining of a headache, and his face was twisted, with frothy secretions drooling from his mouth,” she replied.

I asked her about her husband’s past medical problems. She told me that he has high blood pressure but does not take his medications regularly.

She tops off her comments by saying, “The most careless and irresponsible bloke. I should not have married him.”

I looked at her and found her staring at her dying husband with contempt and hate, no hint of compassion or concern in her demeanor — a classic example of a toxic marriage with a bitter, unhappy, and frustrated partner. There is a pin-drop silence in the examination room. Finally, I say, “Ma’am, you are not helping your husband.”

She angrily looks at me and blurted out, “How long do I have to stay here?” Her answer surprised me, and I said, “We would like you to stay until I get the CT scan report back. The scan will tell us whether your husband will need surgical intervention, and, in that situation, we will need you to sign the consent forms for the treatment.”

She gets upset and wants to leave right away. I looked at Nurse Brenda, and she tells me that if she wants to abandon her husband, we have no control over this situation.

I looked at her and advised her to stay, but she was adamant about her decision. I finally asked her, "What is so urgent that you would leave your husband in such a precarious situation?" Her reason for leaving her dying husband was the most shocking and upsetting to me because I was not exposed to this side of British culture.

She said, "My dog is home alone. I cannot leave my poor dog sitting alone and suffering. You people have my telephone number, and if you need my consent, I can give it to you over the telephone." She slammed the door shut and left the emergency room.

We did not have to bother her; because her husband had a cardiac arrest and passed away during the CT scan.

The patient died alone while his wife refused to stay by his side. She was more worried about her dog. This was a huge cultural shock for me. I remembered the Indian patient, whose wife sold her precious jewelry to save him. How my mom sold her gold coins and sacrificed her dreams so that her son could fulfill his dreams.

Suddenly, I realized how different Indian culture was from English culture. I felt like I had landed on an alien island where I must learn more than postgraduate medicine.

Western culture has its specific perspectives and practices that suit its land and lifestyle. Each culture, whether Indian or British, is unique and beautiful in its own way. My goal was to choose the right elements—picking pearls from British culture and incorporating them into my life.

After finishing the internship, I was ready to move forward. I planned to pursue postgraduate training by applying to the Foundation Program. The Foundation Program is a bridge between undergraduate training in medicine and training in a specialty.

I applied and got the interview at Peterborough General Hospital—the happiest day of my life. The hospital was a teaching hospital located in Peterborough in Eastern London. The town is famous for its 12th-century Peterborough Cathedral with the Gothic façade. I shared this good news with my friend and mentor, Dr. Andrew Pembroke, and asked for his help and guidance to prepare for this once-in-a-lifetime opportunity. He helped me pick out a nice white linen shirt with a matching blue blazer and pants.

This ego-busting interview preparation almost ate up all my savings. After a month of academic preparation and learning the proper British mannerisms, I was ready—partly excited, partly scared. Andrew dropped me at the railway station and wished me good luck.

I entered the large meeting room, which had a mahogany table and heavy, cushioned leather chairs. The Chief of the Department of Medicine, Dr. Steve Pilcher, welcomed me with a broad grin. He pointed to the chair and said, "Please have a seat, Dr. B.....shi." He was having a hard time pronouncing my name—a bad start for a candidate.

Dr. Pilcher was a heavy-set man with a ruddy complexion and a short, stubby nose supporting thick-rimmed brown glasses—the typical face of the guy who loves his drinks. Sitting next to Dr. Pilcher was a much younger-looking junior doctor. He introduced himself. He was a Registrar doing post-graduation.

Dr. Pilcher opens my file, and after flipping through some pages, he closes it. He says, "Dr. B., what was your main purpose in coming to the UK from India?" This question shakes me up, and before answering, I look up and see both Dr. Pilcher and the Registrar staring at me through their thick glasses with a stupid grin. I thought I did not hear him well, and I said, "Excuse me." His Registrar repeats the question.

I said, "Sir, the British government is advertising and recruiting Indian doctors to work in the National Health Service. I decided to come here to continue my post-graduation studies." Dr. Pilcher says, "You could have done the post-graduation in India." I say, "Sir, I did not have the resources to continue my studies in India."

He continues, "What are you planning to do after post-graduation? Are you going to go back to India or stay in England?" He speaks with the demeanor of a man who thinks that he is God's gift to mankind—arrogant and not a whiff of humility.

I look at him and see an old, frustrated, bitter man. Old age has not tenderized him. In his eyes, I see no respect for me. He failed to see me as a human being.

He was incapable of understanding the dreams of a poor kid. I was an entity, and he had every God-given right to trample on my self-respect and dignity.

My demeanor must have told him that I was done with his insults. I said, "Sir, you selected me for this interview and I hoped you would test my medical knowledge. Whether I will stay in the UK or return to India is not the front-burner issue for me. I thought you would look at my credentials and decide whether I was qualified for the post-graduation slot. Since the beginning of this interview, you have not asked me a single medical question. This meeting looks more like a police interrogation, as if I have committed a crime by coming to England."

Dr. Pilcher was surprised to hear my response to his behavior. I thought he was a sadist who would call foreign students for a fake interview to enjoy his afternoon. Finally, I said, "Sir, I was well prepared for this interview. I am disappointed and sorry that I came here." That was the end of the interview and the end of my dreams of continuing my post-graduation in England. I concluded that the U.K. was not the country for me to grow and evolve as a physician.

Journey Continues

After this nerve-racking and humiliating interview, I came back to London. I was disappointed and hurt. I saw my dreams of becoming a specialist go up in smoke. It was a British colonizer mindset — a way of thinking, valuing, feeling, and behaving that reflects dominance over Indians. It was not a lack of desire and will on my part. It was the English mindset — a stumbling block for achieving my goal.

Dr. Pembroke was anxiously waiting to hear about my interview. I told him how badly Dr. Pilcher treated me. He was shocked but not surprised, because it was not the first time he had seen the hypocrisy and subtle racism in his country.

Dr. Pembroke knew I was hurting, and to cheer me up, he invited me to join him and his girlfriend for a beer and cucumber sandwich. After a glass of cold lager, I felt better. After we finished eating, I was unusually quiet; the pain and humiliation I suffered during the interview were still simmering in my heart.

Dr. Pembroke said, "Bhikshu, can I give you brotherly advice?"

I looked up and saw him looking at me with a pensive demeanor. He was worried that his comments might hurt me more than heal my pain. He was a reserved and thoughtful man who was very frugal with his words. I always respected his opinion.

In a low tone, almost a whisper, he said, "You should leave England — the post-graduate education infrastructure in England is not in favor of foreign doctors."

"I cannot go back to India without post-graduation," I said.

He said, "Leave England and emigrate to the USA."

Dr. Pembroke had been to the USA, and after his fellowship, he decided to return to England. He told me the only reason he came back was to take care of his mentally retarded older brother.

This meeting was a watershed event in my life. Dr. Pembroke became my mentor and guide in helping me to emigrate.

After my interview with Dr. Pilcher, I was depressed and thought this was the end of my journey. My innate optimistic attitude towards life started changing into a deep sense of failure and an inferiority complex. With Dr. Pembroke's support, a deep burning desire to do post-graduation was rekindled.

In life, we should never pigeonhole people. It is wrong to judge people. Not everybody is racist in England; Dr. Pilcher and Dr. Pembroke are different faces of the same coin. Every crisis in life also has a hidden opportunity. When one door closes, another door opens

— but unfortunately, we keep looking at the closed door and think that it is the end of our journey.

I took the risk. I left my family and the security of my home to try my luck in a foreign land to fulfill my deeply desired mission.

When we take risks, we will face failure. But what happens afterward is defining. A failure does not have to be a failure at all if we have a rescue plan. My setback in England created a rescue plan — to emigrate to the USA.

To apply for a post-graduation residency program in the USA, you need to be certified by the Education Commission for Foreign Medical Graduates (ECFMG), which is the organization that evaluates whether foreign medical graduates are sufficiently prepared for the U.S. medical residency program. My medical school, where I graduated, was approved by the ECFMG — that means after passing the ECFMG examination, I can continue post-graduation training in the U.S.

To get ECFMG certification, you need to pass the United States Medical Licensing Examination, which tests your medical and clinical knowledge. It was my good luck that I did not have to leave London to take the ECFMG examination. I took the exam at the International Test Center in London and passed with good grades. Part of the credit also goes to Dr. Pembroke, who guided me.

The day I received the ECFMG certificate was the happiest day of my life. For the first time since leaving India, I saw a ray of sunshine in the dark and depressing journey of my life.

The residency program in the USA is the best in the world. It is geared towards training world-class specialists in different fields of medicine and surgery. The teaching program provides comprehensive training within the chosen specialty.

After passing the exam and before starting the residency program, I applied for a visa to enter the USA. My visa interview was the most interesting experience of my life. After leaving India, for the first time, I experienced the genuine kindness and compassion of a person who had the power to decide my destiny.

An elderly white American woman conducted my visa interview. She had sandy curly hair and no make-up. She was wearing a white blouse and a gold chain necklace with a "Cross" peacefully resting in the middle of her chest.

After reviewing my application, she said, "Dr. Bhikshu, you have not indicated what kind of visa you are applying for."

I said, "I want to go to the States for further studies and do post-graduation in medicine. I was not sure what kind of visa I would need."

Her next question surprised me because it was irrelevant to my visa application. She asked, "Are you married?" I replied, "No."

She looked at me and said, "If you enter the States on a student visa, after finishing your studies, you must leave and go back to India. Since you are already a medical doctor, you will be employed by the hospital.

You are qualified to apply for an H1 work visa or a Green Card."

I was quiet and did not know what to pick—H1 visa or Green Card. She understood my dilemma and kept looking at me. Her gaze had a gift of attention, and it communicated her concern about my confusion. She was trying her best to help me pick the correct visa—she was the kind of person who was an illuminator; she showed me the brightness of her care and kindness. She made me feel respected. There was no hostility in her demeanor despite my confusion.

After not getting a proper response from me, she explained that with an H1 visa, if I am not working, I must leave the States, but with a Green Card, I can stay and become a citizen. She continued with her gentle voice, "Since you are not married, it is possible you may meet an American girl and want to get married; in that case, you don't have to leave the country." Finally, she said, "I think you should apply for the Green Card."

I said, "Thanks for your advice and kindness."

She said, "To get a Green Card, you have to show me proof of a bank account with a minimum of 500.00 pounds."

Before my interview with Dr. Pilcher, I had more than 500 pounds in the bank, but buying new clothes burned most of my savings.

I told her that I didn't have 500 pounds.

She said, "In that case, you won't get a Green Card." Before leaving her office, she softly whispered, "Borrow money from your friends and put it in your account." She looked at me with a saintly smile and left the office.

The following week, I went for my second interview. I met her, and after seeing the bank savings book, she approved my application for the Green Card.

She told me to raise my right arm for the "Oath of Allegiance." After this life-changing ceremony, I left the Embassy—a changed person.

I started my internship at the university hospital in Brooklyn, USA. This was the most enjoyable and stable period in my turbulent life. After completion of the post-graduation training program, I would be a specialist. During training, we interns and residents were helping each other to understand and solve the complexities of human diseases—the enigma of different maladies was as alien to us as the topography of an unknown planet.

For a physician, translating book knowledge into hands-on experience is the most challenging part of his evolution. A small mistake or moment of carelessness can have catastrophic consequences for the patient. A physician's mission is to do his work with a highly desirable goal: to achieve a "zero-error" outcome.

A physician needs God's unconditional grace to stay grounded and humble; without these blessings, he may lose the core tenets of his mission.

FATHER GALLAGHER

The Roman Catholic Church defines itself as the "People of God."

During the last year of fellowship training, I was assigned to rotate in a Catholic charity hospital affiliated with my university hospital. I met Father Gallagher for the first time when he was called to perform the "Last Rites," the anointing of the sick, for a patient of mine who was dying from terminal congestive heart failure.

Father was a tall, middle-aged man with well-groomed, shining black hair that parted in the middle. He had an ever-present gentle smile, and the liturgical vestments gave him an aura of divine truth and humility.

When Father entered the room, I saw a unique peace and smile on my dying patient's face. During all the time I spent taking care of him, I had never seen him smile, but a brief visit by Father Gallagher did something different; it healed him. He saw his God through Father Gallagher.

After the prayer, I left the room with Father Gallagher to give the family members privacy to deal with their grief.

I thanked him and said, "Father, your brief visit did more for him than all the medicines I gave him."

Father said, what was holding him back from seeing Jesus was this prayer. Now, after the prayer, his journey would be peaceful.

I did not want Father Gallagher to leave the patient's room unaccompanied. I thought it would be rude not to accompany him to the elevators. This prayer visit created a unique kind of respect and unexplained feelings in my heart.

While waiting for the elevator, Father Gallagher looks at my name tag and surprises me by saying he had met a Bhikshu while growing up in India. After saying that, Father's demeanor changes, and he becomes more reflective. He closes his eyes for a moment, then looks upward and finally at me. He is trying hard to bring out deeply buried memories that are somehow connected to his childhood. It is a well-known medical fact that our eyes (oculomotor neurons) are connected to the memory centers.

I wanted to stimulate a real conversation with Father Gallagher and ask him about his life. I wanted to know more about his life journey. It was a strange coincidence that two kids from different backgrounds, born in India, met in this hospital in the U.S. Was it a coincidence or our destinies that brought us together? We were doing God's job in our own ways. It is said,coincidence is God's way of staying anonymous.

Before getting into the elevator, Father smiled and said, "Dr. Bhikshu, we will continue our conversation another time." The elevator left the floor, and I was still standing there, unable to move. The brief conversation with Father raised so many questions in my mind. I wanted to know more about Father Gallagher. I was looking forward to our next meeting.

Later, talking to Sisters in the hospital, I learned that about five years back, Father had migrated from Ireland. Since joining the hospital, he has lived in a room attached to the hospital's Cancer Unit. The room was big enough to accommodate his bed and reading desk. The hospital offered him private accommodation outside, but he refused. His life was totally dedicated to his church and the patients. He would eat his meals alone in the cafeteria—a simple and frugal lifestyle indicating a true representation of his faith. For Father, simplicity and frugality were the essential elements of his calling.

The next day, I met Father in the employees' cafeteria during lunchtime. After picking up the food, he asked me to join him. Father knew that his comments about meeting Bhikshus in India had raised more questions and curiosity in my mind.

I said, "Father, I am still wondering when you told me you met a boy named Bhikshu in India. Were you born in India?"

He said, "Yes. My dad worked for the British Civil Service. He was posted in Burma, which was part of India. I was born there."

He continued, "The town where we were living was a small town, and most of the inhabitants were Buddhists. On the outskirts of the town, there was an Ashram.

A boy living in the Ashram was called Bhikshu. He was a couple of years older than I."

I said, "You mean, beggar boy?"

Father was surprised to hear 'beggar boy,' and said, "That is not a correct translation of Bhikshu. When we say beggar, we think of a person sitting on the roadside and asking for money.

The Bhikshus are more like monks. They only knock at your door for food, and the rest of the day they spend in the Ashram studying holy scripture and praying. My mom liked him so much that whenever he came to our home for food, she would ask our housemaid to make potato curry for him because he liked it. My dad used to say, "He is one of us because, like the Irish, he is fond of potatoes."

After telling me his life story, Father asked me how I got my name, Bhikshu. I told him how my parents went through all the troubles to have me.

This exchange of our life stories created a special relationship between us. During one of our lunch meetings, I asked, "Father, what made you choose the life you are leading now? As the son of an Irish civil servant, I expected you to follow in your dad's footsteps and work for the British."

He said, "My parents were devout Catholics. The British behavior with Indians was so un-Christian that I decided I would never work for the British. After the independence of India, our family moved back to Ireland. When I learned how badly the British treated the Irish, I hated them more."

Father continued in a pensive demeanor and said, "I did not want to live a life full of bitterness and hatred. While growing up in India, when I saw a Bhikshu boy, I did not see a 'beggar'; what I saw was a unique combination of poverty and spirituality. In Ireland, the British controlled most of the businesses. I could not serve the British and God simultaneously, so I decided to serve God."

"After graduating from high school, I attended the seminary to study theology for six years, and finally, I came to the stage of ordination to live a full, joyful, and happy life as a priest."

I started meeting Father Gallagher more frequently and seeing him as my spiritual guide. Before leaving the hospital, I asked him how to navigate the next chapter of my life journey as a practicing cardiologist entering the "business of medicine." I wanted to know how to balance the complexity of a physician's power with the temptation and greed of money. The unchecked power of physicians during the vulnerable time in a patient's life could corrupt them.

He said, "We must draw a line between greed and aspirations—between bottomless desire for more and human desire to succeed." He continued, "Making money at the cost of your God-given mission should never become a front-burning issue in your life."

Father Gallagher surprised me by giving me a framed copy of the following prayer. This precious gift stayed with me and guided my life as a physician. Doctors are human beings, and they suffer from biases as all humans do.

Daily Prayer of The Physician

Almighty God,

You have created the human body with infinite wisdom.

In Your eternal providence, You have chosen me to watch over the life and health of Your children.

I now commit myself to the duties of my profession. Support me in these great labors so that they may benefit humankind, for without Your help, not even the least of things will succeed.

Inspire me with love for my art and for Your creatures. Do not allow the thirst for profit or the ambition for renown and admiration to interfere with my profession, for these are the enemies of truth and can lead me astray in the great task of caring for the welfare of Your creatures.

Preserve the strength of my body and soul so that they may be ever ready to help—the rich and the poor, the good and the bad, enemy as well as friend. In the sufferer, let me see only the human being.

Almighty God, You have chosen me in Your mercy to watch over the life and death of Your creatures. Support me in this great task so that it may benefit humankind, for without Your help, not even the least thing will succeed.

After meeting Father Gallagher and learning about his life, I saw a true image of the "People of God."

Finally, after completing three years of residency in Internal Medicine and two years of fellowship in Cardiology, I was certified as a Cardiovascular Specialist.

After all these years of pain and humiliation from racial prejudices, I was able to cross the most critical milestone in my life.

India, my motherland, empowered me with the wings of medical education. The U.S., my adopted home, gave me open sky and an unlimited horizon to fly and fulfill my dreams. Finally, the time has arrived to show my gratitude by sincerely and ethically serving the good people of this wonderful land.

Business of Medicine

A brief history of how a noble profession degenerated into its present dysfunctional state and how our heartless capitalism has exploited innocent people at the most vulnerable period in their lives.

The business story of Western medicine starts with John D. Rockefeller. Rockefeller is considered the wealthiest American of all time and the richest person in modern history. He controlled 90% of all petroleum refineries in America. In 1935, Vitamin C became the first vitamin to be artificially synthesized in Switzerland. Rockefeller saw a big opportunity: the possibility that medications could be developed from petroleum byproducts. He saw the chance to monopolize the medical industry.

But there was a big problem with Rockefeller's plan. In 1900, almost half of the medical colleges and doctors in America were practicing holistic medicine, using extensive knowledge from European and Native American traditions.

The history of medicine would be inconceivable without medicinal plants. In India, the Ayurvedic system of medicine developed around 5000 BCE, and it treated most diseases with medicinal plants.

In 1800, prominent doctors treated heart attacks with leeches—**hirudotherapy**. Indeed, by the mid-1800s, the demand for leeches was so high that the French imported about forty million leeches a year for medical purposes. The leeches secrete an anticoagulant known as **hirudin** that prevents blood clotting.

Recombinant technology has developed methods to produce recombinant forms of hirudin (**r-hirudin**) for therapeutic use. In the second half of the 20th century, leeches made a comeback in microsurgery. In 2004, the Food and Drug Administration (FDA) approved the commercial marketing of medicinal leeches because they met the criteria for medical devices.

Rockefeller knew that to gain control of the medical industry, he would have to eliminate unregulated holistic medicine. This was the biggest tragedy in medicine because by destroying holistic medicine, we also destroyed centuries of accumulated knowledge of the medicinal treasures Mother Earth has for us.

In 1910, his contractor, Abraham Flexner, submitted a report to Congress concluding that there were too many doctors and medical schools in America and that all the natural healing modalities that had existed for hundreds of years were unscientific quackery. The report called for the standardization of medical education, whereby only the AMA would be allowed to grant medical school licensure in the USA.

Certainly, Flexner's report did have some valid points, but its motives were entirely driven by Rockefeller's desire for complete control of the medical system—Congress changed laws related to medical practice, and allopathic medicine became a standard modality.

With new laws in place, Rockefeller teamed up with Andrew Carnegie and started funding medical schools all over America on the strict condition that they would only teach allopathic medicine. The previous curriculum of these medical schools was dismantled. Teaching the healing power of herbs, diet, and other (non-drug) treatments was removed entirely from the medical programs. Homeopathy and natural medicines were demonized through the newspapers and other media at the time. Some doctors were even jailed for using natural medicinal treatments, including treatments that had been used safely and effectively for decades before. Allopathic medicine was now defined as a process of prescribing patented drugs. "A PILL FOR AN ILL" became the holy mantra of American medicine.

Rockefeller wasn't just wiping out traditional medicine in America; he saw a bigger market on the other side of the world and wanted to remove traditional Chinese medicine from China. The China Medical Board (CMB) was created in 1914 by the Rockefeller Foundation (RF), which provided a $12 million grant.

Luckily, Rockefeller's mission in China mostly failed, and the practice of traditional Chinese medicine was preserved for centuries to come.

In short, the capitalistic infrastructure built by Rockefeller and Andrew Carnegie is still alive and in use by "Big Pharma"—they make significant donations to medical schools in exchange for advertising their upcoming, expensive medicines. As part of this system, many alternative treatments are criminalized. For example, by law, it is illegal to treat cancer with any modality except chemotherapy, radiation, or surgery—it is actually a criminal felony for medical practitioners to treat cancer with anything but these three modalities. The average cost of cancer treatment is $150,000, so clearly Rockefeller and his predecessors were keen to keep the monopoly on this one. And of course, the American Cancer Society was founded by none other than John D. Rockefeller in 1913.

Patients are treated like customers. We should not be surprised that we are faced with the fact that the cost of medical care in America is rated #1, yet the quality of our medical care is rated #37.

Unfortunately, these natural effects occur when our medicine is run like a mega-corporation instead of a service to the people. —Scientific Research, Western Medicine

Before Medicare was created, approximately 60% of people over the age of 65 had health insurance, which was often unavailable or unaffordable to many others because older adults paid more than three times as much for health insurance as younger people.

Under the leadership of President Lyndon Johnson, Congress enacted Medicare to provide health insurance to people aged 65 and older, regardless of income or medical history. Medicare added the option of payment to HMOs (Health Maintenance Organizations) in 1970. The HMO, a new capitalist baby, was born from the simple and generous mother Medicare; organized greed in the health care industry lives on.

I personally experienced the revenue-maximizing mission of the HMO. After getting a fellowship in cardiovascular diseases, I joined our local HMO to take care of patients with heart problems. This was a staff-model HMO (where patients can receive services only through a limited number of providers) in which physicians are HMO employees. The providers see enrolled members in HMO-owned clinics.

At the end of my one-year contract with the HMO, I received a detailed letter indicating my revenue-generating productivity profile. According to the CFO, I was not generating enough revenue to justify my compensation. The letter ended with the warning: "THE CONTRACT WILL BE TERMINATED IF THERE IS NO IMPROVEMENT IN PRODUCTIVITY."

The CFO, a very pleasant gentleman, met me the next day and explained that I was spending too much time with patients. I was surprised to learn this because all these patients were under the care of the previous cardiologist. I was seeing these patients for the first time. It took more time to evaluate them properly—I spent more than 20 minutes (time allotted) for each patient. While working for the HMO, I learned the facts about physician compensation based on productivity—to pay

8 dollars in compensation, a physician must generate 100 dollars.

Despite my best efforts to see more patients, I was still not generating enough revenue for the HMO. To be more productive, I stopped taking a one-hour lunch break. There were no complaints from patients about medical care and no lawsuit against me, but the CFO still believed that I was a bad investment—a money-losing entity. I was a provider, not a physician.

After six months of observation, my job was terminated, and I was fired. This was a painful experience at the beginning of my professional career. I was worried about my future, but deep down at the core of my consciousness, I was happy and at peace with myself, knowing that I kept my part of the covenant with God and did not compromise the care of my patients.

Our medical profession is a selfless vocation. God calls us to respond freely and generously to His call. It is our covenant with God, not a contract with HMOs.

The survival of our medical profession as intended by God will depend on heeding once again the ancient admonition: I have set before you life and death, blessing and curse. Therefore, choose life, that you and your offspring may live.

After getting fired from the HMO, I had plenty of time to think about the future. During this period of blessed solitude, I had an epiphany that acted like a seed crystal and changed my life as a physician.

What am I going to do with this life? I reflected on the journey of my life and the troubles I went through.

As a kid, I survived the bloody sectarian migration. After migrating from India and crossing two oceans, I finally achieved my goal and became a cardiologist. I thought God wanted me to do something meaningful with my life, and not to become a mule for the profit-making medical organizations. After a brief period of unemployment and reflection, I started looking for a job. I wanted to work for a non-profit hospital serving the rural community.

The rural areas are home to a fifth of Americans. Medical care in these areas is suboptimal and, in some cases, extremely primitive. The cardiovascular mortality in rural areas is about 20% more than in urban areas. It is because of a poor cardiovascular risk profile and limited access to health care.

A community hospital in the heart of West Virginia was searching for a cardiologist. The job description: "to start a Cardiology Department and to manage a state-of-the-art Cardiac Care Unit." After a brief interview with the hospital administrator, I was hired as the Chief of Cardiology. It was a God-sent opportunity. After getting fired from the HMO, my future looked abysmal, and I had no idea in which direction life would go. This new job opportunity solidified my deep-rooted faith in destiny. I realized that the journey of my life was predetermined. As a two-year-old kid, I survived the bloody sectarian partition of India. Finally, I saw the light—the purpose of life's journey: to serve the rural community.

The town where I started the cardiology services was situated about sixty miles from the big city. The town was named after an Indian chief and had a population of 1,500 people. It was located in the beautiful Appalachian Mountains, along the Guyandotte River. It was the hub of the coal industry. The population was mostly white coal miners and mine owners; there were a few Black families.

The hospital was located on the bank of the Guyandotte River and had a capacity of 130 beds. On my first day on the job, Dr. David Morrison, Chief of Medicine, welcomed me with a friendly hug in his office. The office was decorated with coal mine work-related memorabilia, like a bourbon bottle in the shape of a coal miner holding a cage with a canary.

Dr. Morrison, a middle-aged, tall man with a square face and ruddy complexion, had a pleasant demeanor. His friendly hug washed away all my hidden anxiety and nervousness. I saw in his eyes a genuine appreciation of my joining his department. He was a true West Virginian: a sincere, emotionally naked man. His ancestors migrated from Europe and were coal miners. He was the first to go to college, and after finishing an internal medicine residency, he decided to return to his hometown to serve his people. I respected and liked him.

I said, "Dr. Morrison." Before I finished addressing him, he said, "Please call me David, not Dr. Morrison." He erased all the formalities between us and, over time, became my friend and social mentor.

I said, "David, I will need all your help to understand the culture of the people living here. It will help me to take care of heart problems." He was surprised by this question.

After a brief period of silence, he said, "I thought you were going to ask me to give you a big office overlooking the river and other amenities."

I said, "David, as you told me, in this area, more than 50% of patients die after suffering a heart attack. It is important to understand the culture because it will help me to give them proper cardiac care. Getting a fancy big office is the last thing on my mind."

He said, "Tomorrow morning, we will have breakfast together. Meet me in the employees' cafeteria, and that will be the beginning of our cultural education."

The cafeteria breakfast was a cultural shock and an eye-opener. Some of the dishes being served were alien to me. Most of the dishes were full of fat and high in calories. After seeing the breakfast dishes, I was not surprised to learn that, according to the CDC, West Virginia has the highest obesity rate in America, at about 40%.

Every state has certain foods that are unique to that region. People from those states grew up with those foods. Dr. Morrison looked at my face and knew I did not like what I saw. After picking up a boiled egg and a toast, I joined Dr. Morrison.

I said, "David, I was surprised to see what kind of food we are serving to the employees. No wonder we have an epidemic of obesity and heart attacks. We should talk to the administration to see if we can introduce a few healthy dishes."

So, my journey as Chief of Cardiology started from the employee cafeteria. I believe that building a fancy Cardiac Care Unit is not going to reduce cardiac mortality. We must educate people about the role of an unhealthy diet in causing disease. In the beginning, it was more difficult than I thought, but with mandatory classes on nutrition and the introduction of healthy food, over time, I saw employees start picking up healthy dishes—especially whenever they saw me standing in the food line.

Culture is a shortcut for reality. How do you change people's food habits that they have grown up eating all their lives? I wanted to do it slowly. The most important part of learning about the culture was simplifying interactions. Frictionless interaction is key to understanding the core reality of people's culture and way of life.

Before starting the job, I was concerned about whether the people of this town, who had not seen a doctor from India, would accept me to treat their heart problems. This simple act of understanding people's food and culture had far-reaching consequences. The employees appreciated my genuine concern for their health. Once the townspeople learned that I was unmarried and living alone, they started inviting me for dinner. In a couple of months, all my doubts and fears about being a foreign doctor and not being accepted by the people, disappeared.

I told Dr. Morrison about the dinner invitation I received from one of my patients and wanted to know if it was appropriate to accept.

He said he was pleased to hear about the invitation and encouraged me to meet people socially. "This is the best way to learn about the culture and food habits of our people."

The dinner invitation was from the first patient I treated in the new CCU. He was a retired coal miner suffering from black lungs. He suffered a massive heart attack. He was admitted to the CCU, and a few hours after admission, his blood pressure and heart rate dropped. We inserted a temporary pacemaker to stabilize his heart rate, and with a clot-busting drug, he recovered miraculously without much damage to his heart.

In a way, he was lucky the hospital was now equipped to provide him with cardiac services. In the past, when the hospital did not provide cardiac services, the patients were transported on a bumpy, small road to the university hospital, which was about sixty miles away. He would have died if he had been transported to the city hospital and not treated locally.

The dinner was more elaborate than I thought. The family invited relatives and friends to a celebration of life and of a new beginning for my patient. The patient and his family welcomed me with hugs. I saw genuine respect and love in their demeanor.

The house was a log cabin with a large dining area attached to a small kitchen. The aroma of freshly baked biscuits and pinto beans made this humble log cabin heavenly. In the corner, there was a small window decorated with Christmas lights, and resting on the windowsill were Christian icons facing the kitchen. Next to the icons, I saw a glass box labelled "Saint P." In the box, I was surprised to see a metallic wire that looked like a temporary pacemaker. Mr. Atkinson, our patient, was standing behind me with a broad, mysterious grin.

I asked him, "Is this the pacemaker wire?" By now, most of the invited guests had started gathering around us and looking at the glass box.

Mr. Atkinson said, "Yes, thanks for saving my life by regulating the heart with this pacemaker."

He continued, "When I was discharged from the hospital, I asked the head nurse if she could give me the pacemaker wire as a souvenir. She was kind enough to give it to me. She also told me that I was the lucky patient who had the first pacemaker in town and survived."

He continued with a pensive demeanor, "After showing this pacemaker to my priest and congregation, I brought it home, and now I am keeping it with my other saints. This pacemaker reminds me not to forget the dark days in my life."

I loved Mr. Atkinson's sense of humor. The heart attack was a watershed event in his life. It would have killed him. He was coping with this traumatic event by reaching out to friends and making a mockery of the monstrous heart attack.

Mr. Atkinson's next comment surprised me: "Our Lord, Jesus, after resurrection still had stigmata; to teach us not to forget our sufferings and dark days in life. Seeing this pacemaker and not forgetting the dark days in my life is my way of following the teachings of our Lord."

Mr. Atkinson, a simple man, had no formal education. He worked as a coal miner and lived all his life in this small town. His interpretation of the teachings of the Bible touched me deeply, and I developed a special kind of love and respect for him. His narrative about Christ's wounds after resurrection helped him to bend the redemptive arc toward healing from brokenness. He taught me more about the core of Christianity than all the sermons I had heard before.

After hearing Mr. Atkinson's comments on the resurrection of the wounded Jesus, I remembered reading about "the Japanese tradition of Kintsugi."

Kintsugi is the art of repairing broken pottery pieces with lacquer dusted with gold. A Kintsugi master will make broken pottery even more visibly sophisticated and beautiful. No traumas in life are alike, and similarly, no broken pottery looks the same. The work done by Kintsugi masters is built on the idea that embracing traumas and imperfections can help us learn and become better people. Each piece of broken pottery, when restored by the Kintsugi master, is different and more sophisticated than its original form.

For the victims of trauma to recover, they should not be told to forget their traumas; they need to find ways to integrate them into their life stories. It is part of their story—never to be downplayed—but it need not define who they are perpetually. The wounds of Jesus are not the final words, but they are meaningful.

If Jesus showed us his scars even after his resurrection, then maybe we can learn to integrate pain and suffering into our lives in a way that frees us from wasting energy spent in denial. It is through our brokenness that God's grace can shine.

19th-century hymn,
"Crown Him with Many Crowns"

Crown Him the Lord of Love,
Behold his hand and side,
Rich wounds yet visible above,
In beauty glorified:
No angel in the sky
Can fully bear that sight,
But downward bends his burning eyes
At mysteries so bright.
Our wounds will not be left in the grave,
but also in beauty glorified.
Our griefs, betrayals, and disabilities
are so much a part of who we are
that they will not be discarded and left behind.
They will become essential
to the beauty that awaits us.
—"The Jesus Who Was Still Wounded After
Resurrection,"
New York Times

The family dining table was covered from end to end with different dishes. I was able to figure out some dishes, like beans and rice, but could not figure out the meat dishes.

Mrs. Atkinson introduced me to the meat dishes and said, "Before getting sick, her husband hunted a deer and a couple of rabbits."

She continued, "If our leaders take away our guns, we will be eating pinto beans and cornbread all the time. I hope the liberals stop their campaign against gun possession."

Mrs. Atkinson was making a valid argument about the possession of guns. In the rural areas, guns are not used to commit crimes and kill people. Most people use guns to hunt or protect themselves from wild animals.

While living in New York, I had a myopic view of gun possession. I always associated guns with crimes. This was not the view of rural America.

I was grateful to Dr. Morrison for his encouragement to meet the town people socially and understand their culture. The dinner with Mr. Atkinson was the beginning of my cultural education.

Culture plays a huge role in medical interactions. Since I was brought up in a different culture from my patients, I must understand their culture to take care of them properly. To achieve this objective, after the cardiac examination, I would ask the patients about non-medical issues facing their lives. The bone-crushing poverty, partially created by the capitalistic mindset of coal mine owners, was the root cause of their suffering.

It was ironic that I started my medical profession taking care of poor people in India and most likely would end my career taking care of poor people in the U.S.

My new office is on the third floor next to the newly constructed C.C.U. It has a panoramic view overlooking the Guyandotte River, with rolling hills touching the horizon. The office is decorated with paintings of coal miners in different scenarios. A large mahogany table with a leather chair is on the opposite side of a bow window. The hospital must have spent a lot of money on the office, and I loved it.

The patients take the hospital elevator to come for the examination. I was surprised to learn that many patients feared getting in the elevator and preferred to take the stairs. Most of my patients with heart conditions were also suffering from black lungs, and climbing stairs was making them sicker. I felt guilty whenever I saw a patient huffing and puffing while climbing the stairs, and I decided to move my office to the ground floor.

I met Dr. Morrison in the hall and said, "I want to move my office to the ground floor."

He was surprised because the hospital had spent a good amount of money fixing up the office in the perfect location. This was Dr. Morrison's idea because he wanted to keep me happy by giving me the best office in the hospital.

After a brief pause, he asked, "Why?"

I said, "Dr. Morrison, as you know, most people in the town have not used the elevator in their lives. The patients are hesitant to take the elevator and use the stairs to come to the office.

They should not be climbing three stories to see me." I continued, "One of these days, a patient will suffer a heart attack while climbing the stairs to see me. Before that happens, I would rather move to the ground floor."

I looked up and saw Dr. Morrison leaning back with his arms behind his head, looking at me with a pensive and reflective demeanor. He never expected someone to give up the luxury of working in such a beautiful office.

Finally, he got up from his chair, circled around the large table, came to my side, grabbed me by the arms, gave me a warm, fatherly hug, and said, "We are glad to have you here."

My decision to change my office was a watershed event for my job. The medical staff developed a special regard for my sincere mission to take care of patients, and any doubt in their minds that I came here to have an easy life vanished. I did not accept this job to have an easy life.

The life problems the patients were facing in a small rural town were mind-boggling. Apart from heart disease and poverty, the black lungs were creating havoc in patients' lives.

In the old times, life in the coal mines was slavery by another name. The miners worked 12-hour shifts in harsh and sometimes hazardous conditions, working underground in dark, cramped, dusty, wet, and cold tunnels. Before electricity, miners worked standing in water, swinging their sharp pickaxes and shoveling coal in the flickering light of their gas headlights.

Well into the 20th century, coal miners brought canaries into coal mines as an early warning signal for toxic gases, primarily carbon monoxide—a colorless, odorless gas. The bird, being more sensitive, would become sick before the miners. This was a warning to the miners to leave the mine. The use of canaries in coal mines ended in 1968, about two years after I arrived in the town.

Overall, Black Lung disease is caused by long-term inhalation and deposition of coal dust in the lungs. It decreases life expectancy by about 13 years. In severe Black Lung disease with scarring, oxygen may be prevented from reaching the blood. This results in low oxygen levels, which puts stress on the heart.

The work environment contributes to community health—an unhealthy work environment will lead to diseases. Since coal mining was the major employer in this town, most of my patients were suffering from Black Lung of different severities.

As I started taking care of patients, it became clear that a huge psycho-social component was complicating the clinical symptoms of cardiac maladies. At times, the classical symptoms of a disease would be masked by the patient's mindset.

Cabin Fever

A physician should maintain a time-honored Hippocratic approach to methodical history taking when consulting with a patient. This approach should be extended to include questions about occupation and psychosocial environment.

During our medical training, we did not learn about cabin fever because it is not a medically defined condition but a "folk syndrome." It is a psychological syndrome a person may experience when confined to their homes for a long period.

As winter approaches, I start seeing more patients with heart problems. While talking to them during the examination, I learned about cabin fever—a new complaint I had not heard while working in New York City.

Cabin fever is a psychological syndrome a person may experience when confined to their homes for long periods. It can cause distressing irritability, restlessness, palpitations, and chest pain.

Most of my patients were living uphill in the mountains and were isolated and cut off from modern civilization. There were no proper roads to travel during winter. I saw people buying and loading their vehicles with sacks of pinto beans and rice.

I asked one of my patients, "Why are you buying such a huge quantity of beans and rice?" He replied, "I don't know how much the winter snow will be coming from heaven. It might be three months before I can come down the mountain and buy food."

This kind of social isolation and winter depression, along with structural heart problems, was making them sicker.

After consulting with Dr. Morrison and the hospital administration, I started a special kind of cardiac rehabilitation program called "The Happy Cabin Rehab." After discharge from the CCU, the patients, who were living in isolated, remote places, spent two weeks in the "Happy Cabins." During their stay, the patients were educated about a healthy diet and kept busy with different activities.

After finishing the rehab stay, the patients were assigned volunteers from the church to visit them every two weeks to help them socially integrate with the congregation. A few of my patients joined the Happy Cabin volunteer group and started taking care of other patients.

"Thousands of candles can be lit from a single candle,
and the life of the candle will not be shortened.
Happiness never decreases by being shared."
—Buddha

For my patients who were suffering from cabin fever, antidepressants were not the answer. What was missing in their lives was friendship and social integration. The "Happy Cabin Rehab Center" created a healing environment for the patients.

Social integration is defined by the ways different groups come together to form a whole society. We human beings thrive in a supportive okenvironment. We are innately social animals, and we need other human beings to reaffirm our existence.

Social integration and satisfying relationships not only make people happy but are also associated with better health and even longer lives. People who are more socially connected are at reduced risk for earlier death from all causes, including cardiovascular diseases.

As the Jackson Heart Study has shown, the benefit of social integration in reducing cardiovascular disease was seen in all groups. The association between social integration and mortality did not differ by sex, age, education, or income, suggesting that social integration may be an essential psychosocial asset that promotes health regardless of race/ethnicity or demography. Women who were socially integrated had a more than 3-fold lower risk of suicide over 18 years of follow-up (JAMA). It creates a more stable, safe, and just society for all.

As we see, social integration is a wonderful tool for better health and living longer. It is a low-cost health equalizer in the healthcare inequality between rich and poor. Modern digital society is making us lonely and depressed. There is a big hole in our social fabric.

The American Psychiatric Society says that 25% of U.S. residents are lonely. According to the U.S. Surgeon General's report, lack of social connection currently affects more Americans than, say, diabetes or obesity.

As research in loneliness has shown, when talking about loneliness, what we are talking about are all the issues that swirl perilously underneath it: alienation and isolation, distrust and disconnection, leading to a higher rate of suicides.

As post-war America became more prosperous, this prosperity encouraged people to start owning more things. Every possession comes with a specific headache and anxiety, creating a stressful lifestyle. FOMO eventually made us lonely and isolated.

The things we need and do not have are stressful, but equally stressful is to possess something that we do not need."

According to an article published in *The Journal of Research in Personality*, under the evolutionary theory of loneliness, "Early hominins, outgunned by all manner of long-tooth beasts and without natural armor, achieved safety through community—they learned to work together and form alliances. Our brain evolved to prioritize togetherness and, conversely, to generate an anxiety response when we fail to find it."

With our default mode of living, we are losing the art of analog living—a lifestyle emphasizing slower, simpler, and unplugged living. Physical proximity is not the answer to our loneliness; what matters is our emotional proximity to our community and loved ones.

"Clinical Medicine - A Time Tested Tool"

Clinical medicine reflects the complex nature of the relationship between doctors and patients. It is a slow evolution, and it takes many years for doctors to learn the art of clinical medicine—the practice and study of medicine based on the direct examination of the patient.

Despite the expansion of and remarkable advances in the biomedical sciences and technologies, the multilayered complexities of disease processes, and the ever-changing environments of sick patients, the art of clinical medicine remains very much a mix of physicians' diagnostic capabilities for both curing and healing their patients. This is the time-tested tool that guides a physician, especially when he is taking care of patients without the help of modern diagnostic technology.

Our hospital did not have the modern basic cardiac testing machines to take care of complicated heart attacks. My medical training in India and London equipped me to take care of these patients. It was clinical medicine—the most important tool I had to take care of patients.

Since most of my patients in the town were suffering from Black Lungs, a minor heart attack in these patients was mushrooming into a life-threatening, complicated disease. The black lungs were changing the clinical presentation and trajectory of heart attacks.

My encounter, as a cardiologist, with this deadly combination of a black lung and heart attack was the nerve-racking experience of my life. While taking care of these patients, I realized how years of exposure to work toxins change the natural history of a disease. I had not taken care of patients with severe black lungs and heart attacks while working in New York City. My dilemma was a classic example of learning on the job. However, when we are dealing with a life-threatening situation, we do not have the luxury of a second chance.

My first patient with severe black lung disease and a heart attack was a 60-year-old man who presented to the Emergency Department complaining of persistent right-sided chest pain, cough, and shortness of breath despite being on home oxygen for black lung disease. The chest pain was pleuritic in nature. Since yesterday, he had been feeling heaviness in the middle of his chest; he felt as if an elephant were sitting on his chest. He had no fever or chills.

He smoked 2 packs of cigarettes for many years but quit smoking after he was diagnosed with black lung disease. He was totally disabled, and most of his day was spent hooked up to home oxygen equipment. He had unintentionally lost about 30 lbs.

On examination, I found a dehydrated and cachectic white male with thinning blond hair and hazel, sunken eyes with dilated pupils. He had labored breathing and was profusely diaphoretic. He was very anxious and constantly turning and tossing in the bed, looking for a comfortable spot so he could breathe easily. His wife, who appeared to be much younger, stood beside him, holding his hand and looking worried.

I entered the examination room with the nurse, and before I asked him about his medical history, he said, "Doc, I am drowning, I can't breathe, please do something about it." His electrocardiogram showed that he had suffered an acute myocardial infarction. His blood oxygen saturation dropped to 70% despite oxygen treatment.

The hospital did not have an echocardiogram machine to evaluate his heart function and see how much heart damage there was—and, more importantly, how much decreased heart function was contributing to his shortness of breath. Since he had black lung disease, listening to and examining his lungs was not helping me differentiate how much the heart attack was contributing to his breathing difficulty. During a heart attack, the heart's pumping function decreases, and there is a drop in cardiac output. The heart is not able to pump effectively, and fluid backs up in the lungs. It is called congestive heart failure, and the patient feels like he is drowning. His chest X-ray showed extensive fibrosis and congestion.

Initially, he was treated with IV diuretic, and we increased oxygen inhalation treatment to 100%. This combination did not improve his symptoms, and he became more restless. His cardiac monitor started indicating frequent irregular heartbeats. The low oxygen level in the blood was making the heart attack worse.

It was not a normal clinical response, and it shattered my initial evaluation that I was dealing with a garden-variety minor heart attack. Apart from clinical evaluation, no diagnostic tools were available to diagnose the patient's life-threatening disease. The combination of heart attack and black lung disease mushroomed into a more serious condition called Acute Respiratory Distress Syndrome (ARDS).

This was a highly unusual clinical presentation of a small Inferior Wall Myocardial Infarction that I was seeing for the first time in my life. The minor heart attack caused acute exacerbation of black lung emphysema to ARDS, leading to life-threatening hypoxia.

The patient had been living with black lungs for many years. Before the heart attack, his medical condition was stable. This minor heart attack unraveled the illusion of stability—a classical example of organized instability, where a minor adverse event can shatter the illusion of stability. The patient was caught in a vicious cycle: work environment → black lungs → heart attack → ARDS → hypoxia, causing life-threatening heart complications.

The main culprit in this situation was ARDS, causing hypoxia—low blood oxygen.

'ARDS - A Hidden Monster'

It is a life-threatening condition. It causes poor oxygenation and non-compliant or stiff lungs. There is an extensive degree of pulmonary congestion and damage to the pulmonary vasculature and alveoli. It carries a high mortality rate, and few therapeutic modalities exist to treat this condition.

The patient with ARDS usually starts complaining of worsening shortness of breath that escalates within a few hours into full-blown pulmonary congestion requiring mechanical ventilation. Despite 100% oxygen inhalation, patients still have low blood oxygen levels.

This was the clinical presentation of my patient. Assessing the heart function is crucial to differentiate ARDS from congestive heart failure or to understand the heart failure contribution to ARDS. In big city hospitals, several different diagnostic modalities are available to help the treating physicians understand the underlying pathophysiology. In our small rural hospital, I did not have access to a simple modality like an echocardiogram to take care of this patient.

The management of patients to correct underlying hypoxia in ARDS is a complex process, and it requires special expertise to regulate the flow of oxygen from a ventilator. Most patients with ARDS are treated with Positive End-Expiratory Pressure (PEEP) to keep the collapsed lungs inflated while oxygen flows through the ventilator. Mechanical ventilation with PEEP was the only option I had to save this patient.

There is a fine balance between PEEP pressure and oxygenation. Too high PEEP pressure can worsen baseline oxygen saturation and make the patient sicker. I needed a pulmonologist's consultation to regulate PEEP pressure while I was managing a patient's heart attack, but the hospital did not have a full-time pulmonologist. Our hospital had outpatient services for visiting pulmonologists.

My clinical evaluation was the only tool I had to treat the patient. I had limited clinical exposure to ARDS patients. During my Internal Medicine residency, I took care of a few ARDS patients under the guidance and supervision of a pulmonologist.

In a big city hospital, this patient would have been under the care of multiple specialists, but here I was taking care of him alone with limited resources. The patient's prognosis was guarded, and there was a good chance that I might lose him. This was the ground reality of my predicament, and I had no other option but to do my best. But deep down, at the core of my consciousness, I was aware of my limitations—and scared.

Owning limitations is our road to intellectual humility, which includes an accurate assessment of one's abilities. Intellectual humility tenderizes us and guides us not to set unattainable goals. An intellectually humble person will be more likely to be attentive to their limitations and deeply care about the consequences of their decisions.

Before putting the patient on the ventilator, I asked the head nurse, Jackie, to accompany me to a family meeting and get consent for the ventilator. Under the circumstances, and knowing the patient's advanced lung disease, it was possible that the patient—once put on a ventilator—might need it for the rest of his remaining life.

Jackie was a very pleasant middle-aged person. She had short blond hair and an ever-present smile regardless of the situation in the ER. She was famous for her working mantra: "If it can be fixed, I will fix it." She was born in the same hospital, and after graduating from nursing school, she decided to come back and serve the community. She knew most of the patients coming to the ER by their first names. Her ancestors immigrated from Germany, and after a brief stay in Pennsylvania, they migrated to West Virginia.

I was new in this town and needed moral support, and having someone like Jackie was comforting.

As we entered the meeting room, I found it packed with relatives. They were standing and anxiously waiting to hear about the patient's condition. Jackie took control of the meeting and said, "Please sit down." We all sat down in a semicircle format. Jackie introduced me in her typical informal way, saying, "Mrs. Miller, Dr. B. is taking care of your husband, and he would like to discuss Mr. Miller's medical condition."

I see Mrs. Miller is holding Jackie's hand as if preparing herself to hear the bad news. She knows that her husband is sick, bedridden for the last many years, and now he has suffered a heart attack—and it would be a miracle if he survives this. I was a stranger to them, but Jackie knew most of Mr. Miller's family members, and she was kind of an anchor for them to hold on to at this time of grief.

Before starting my meeting with the family members, even in my heart, I knew that Mr. Miller was in critical condition. I still wanted to give them hope because I believe that while discussing the prognosis of a life-threatening disease, conveying hope is essential. In our discussion with patients, there should be a healthy balance between hope and reality. The patients come to doctors for help—but also for hope. Hope does not require any action at all; it is passive, but it requires very active listeners. Sincere communication between physician and patient has its vibrations, and this has a calming effect on the patient and his loved ones.

I said, "Mr. Miller suffered a heart attack, and under normal conditions, it would be classified as a minor heart attack, but due to Mr. Miller's Black Lung disease, it has dropped the blood oxygen level to a very low level. Even after giving him 100% oxygen and diuretics, we are not able to bring up the blood oxygen level, and it is causing more heart damage."

I continued, "In this situation, our best option is to put him on a ventilator and see how his lungs recover. We don't have a lung specialist, but we have a respiratory therapist who will assist me in regulating the ventilator pressure."

There was pin-drop silence, and then his brother asked, "Since there is no lung specialist, can we take him to Charleston Memorial Hospital?"

I said, "As you know, Charleston Memorial Hospital is a big hospital with lots of specialists to take care of patients, and I would like Mr. Miller to be transferred. But Charleston is about 60 miles from our town, and as you know, there is only a one-lane road to travel on. Under the best road traffic conditions, it will take the ambulance more than an hour to reach Charleston. Mr. Miller has a low blood oxygen level, which is not improving with 100% oxygen inhalation, and on top of that, he suffered a heart attack. In my opinion, he is not fit to be transferred to Charleston Memorial Hospital. It will be dangerous, and we may lose him before he reaches Charleston."

Mr. Miller's brother had more questions, but Mrs. Miller interrupted him and said, "Dr. B., I appreciate your humility and trust your judgment about the transfer. I would like you to take care of my husband, and I will do my part to go to church. I pray to God to be your helping hand."

I said, "Mrs. Miller, in my line of profession, I need all the help I can get."

As we were coming out of the meeting room, Jackie told me, "Dr. B., the ventilator in the Emergency Department is being used, and we don't have an extra ventilator for Mr. Miller."

This was the most shocking news because I had just given Mrs. Miller a glimmer of hope about her husband surviving the heart attack. I stopped walking and looked at Jackie in disbelief, as if it were her fault that the hospital was not equipped to take care of complicated patients. There was no doubt in my mind that without the help of a ventilator, Mr. Miller would not leave the hospital alive.

My demeanor was as if somebody had hit me on the head with a brick. Jackie held my hand and said, "Doc, don't forget you are in a small hospital right in the heart of West Virginia, and not in New York City. I will do my best to arrange a ventilator."

As Jackie and I stand in the corridor trying to figure out how to get a ventilator, Dr. Morrison walks toward us and asks, "Is there a problem?"

I said, "Dr. Morrison, we urgently need a ventilator to save Mr. Miller."

I gave him a brief medical history of Mr. Miller's condition. After listening to the story, to my surprise, he left us without saying a word.

Jackie went to her office to call the ICU to see if a ventilator was available, and I went back to the patient's room.

Mr. Miller's condition was getting worse, and his heart was becoming irregular due to hypoxia. Mr. Miller briefly opened his eyes and looked at me as if saying goodbye, and I stood there helplessly, watching him die.

At that moment, I reflected upon my decision to accept the job and come to a small rural hospital. My coming here had raised people's hope and expectations of getting well when they had heart problems. I thought working without proper equipment would be more harmful to the patients. It would unnecessarily delay the transfer of sick patients to the city hospital. While working in a big city, I was unaware of how much discrepancy there was in medical technology between rural and city hospitals.

During a heart attack, time is the most precious commodity—wasting time to get the proper equipment will cause irreversible damage to the heart, and that will adversely affect the long-term prognosis of heart patients.

While reflecting on my dilemma—should I stay here or leave the town and go back to New York—I saw Dr. Morrison entering the room with the respiratory therapist and ventilator. This unexpected turn of events infused a shot of optimism into the situation. I thanked Dr. Morrison for his timely help.

After sedation, the patient was intubated and put on PEEP. Once his vital signs stabilized, he was transferred to the CCU.

Dr. Morrison invited me to join him for a cup of coffee. I accepted the invitation because I wanted to have a frank discussion with him about the emergency room's lack of equipment to treat sick cardiac patients.

After sitting down with a cup of coffee, I asked Dr. Morrison how he managed to secure the ventilator, and I appreciated his help in saving the patient.

He said, "I requested the surgeon in the operating room to cancel the elective surgery. This was the only way to get the ventilator."

I complimented him and said, "Dr. Morrison, the hospital hired me to take care of heart patients, but without proper equipment, I will be doing a disservice to my patients. So, I need your help to get me a few basic machines to evaluate and treat patients the way they should be treated."

I wanted to share with Dr. Morrison my observation about a unique clinical presentation of a few patients who had Black Lung disease and, on top of that, suffered a heart attack.

I said, "Dr. Morrison, I'm surprised to see a complicated clinical presentation of patients who are coming to the emergency room with a minor heart attack and end up with ARDS. While working in New York City, I have taken care of many patients with chronic lung disease and heart attacks, but these patients did not go into ARDS. It is not the heart, but the ARDS, that is killing the patients—especially when they are being transferred to Charleston Medical Center. I can't imagine how a patient with ARDS will survive the trip to Charleston."

I concluded by saying, "In a few patients who are suffering from Black Lungs, even a minor heart attack is fatal. We must stop transferring these patients to the city hospital. We must take care of them right here in the emergency room, and to take care of them properly, I will need a ventilator and an echocardiogram machine."

I saw Dr. Morrison listening to the problems in a pensive and receptive mood. When we made eye contact, I saw a sincere display of concern in his eyes about his patients. He wanted to protect his patients from dying while being transferred to the city hospital.

This honest, nonverbal communication between the Chief of Medicine and me was the watershed event in my decision to stay and continue caring for the patients. We concluded our meeting when Dr. Morrison said, "Let me work on the administration to get you the necessary equipment."

Mr. Miller's recovery from ARDS was remarkable. Once the blood oxygen level improved, the heart rhythm normalized. The small amount of diuretic did wonders, getting rid of extra fluid from his lungs. The increase in urine output was the most important sign of a patient's recovery and good prognosis.

After three days of close cardiac monitoring and medicines, he was taken off the ventilator. The rest of his stay in the hospital was unremarkable. After a week of low-intensity physical therapy, he was ready to be discharged to continue home physiotherapy.

On the day of discharge, Mrs. Miller brought cake and cookies for the nursing staff. She asked the head nurse if I could see her before she took her husband home.

I entered the meeting room and found it packed with relatives. The air in the room had an entirely different ambience than the first meeting I had with the family. The room felt like it was bubbling with trust and respect for me. Mrs. Miller got up and hugged me, saying, "Dr. B, thanks for saving my husband. I am glad that I trusted your judgment and did not take my husband to Charleston Hospital."

Trust is at the heart of every physician-patient relationship. It is more than medical degrees hanging on the office walls. It is your sincere commitment to the well-being of your patients that creates trust.

A physician's concern for his patient has unique vibrations and energy that the patient can feel, and this force creates an element of trust between patient and physician.

As a physician, your commitment to making ethical decisions based on your patient's best interest is one of the fundamental elements in establishing and maintaining trust. When you are vulnerable, it is safe and easy for the person to exploit that vulnerability.

I said, "Mrs. Miller, I am new in town, and our first meeting—what made you trust me?" I wanted to explore and understand how we human beings judge a person to be trustworthy or not.

She said, "I saw in your eyes a sincere concern for my husband's life, and how you agonized over the decision about transporting him to the city hospital. Last year, his cousin had the same problem, and he died on his way to the city hospital."

Our eyes are windows to nonverbal, trustworthy communication. Mrs. Miller saw in my eyes what I saw in Dr. Morrison's eyes: a sincere effort to help the vulnerable.

It showed that we human beings are connected at the core of our subconscious level, irrespective of our background. According to estimates, only 5% of human brain activity is at the conscious level. The remaining 95% takes place subconsciously, and not only do we have no control over it, but we are also not aware that it is taking place. As Carl Jung proposed, the idea of collective universal subconsciousness suggests a level of interconnectedness through shared human experiences. This unique bonding serves an evolutionary advantage to us humans. It is innate and inherited—a byproduct of our evolution.

It exerts an overwhelming influence on individuals' minds. At times, the subconscious can be terrifying, but it can also heal.

At the end of our meeting, Mrs. Miller said, "We are going to celebrate my husband's new life. I want you to be our guest of honor."

She continued, "Jackie, the head nurse, told us how you guys were struggling to get the ventilator for my husband, so we decided to donate a ventilator to the hospital."

The turn of events—from nearly losing Mr. Miller due to a lack of a ventilator, to his going home and his family donating a ventilator to the hospital—solidified my resolve to stay and continue taking care of patients. I always believed that if our intentions are sincere in our mission in life, then some "Unidentified Force" helps us to achieve our objectives. I came to this hospital with sincere intentions, and this incident validated my belief. It is the sincerity of our intentions, not the lack of resources, that defines the trajectory of your mission.

I decided never to entertain the notion of leaving this town. The only way I can stay true to my mission to take care of patients is to buy a small house near the hospital and live the rest of my life here.

My decision to buy the house burned the psychological bridge that was tempting me to return to New York City.

Oligarchic Capitalism

"Over the centuries, the central indictment of capitalism has remained remarkably consistent: that it is soulless, exploitative, inequitable, unstable and destructive, yet also all conquering and overwhelming."
—John Cassidy

Mr. and Mrs. Miller's dinner invitation, hand-delivered to the office by his brother in my honor, was an eye-opening event because, while living in New York City, I never understood how capitalism works. Capitalism was just an empty word in my vocabulary without real-world implications. The best way to understand this complex economic system is to look at it in small-town settings.

Our town is located on the bank of the Guyandotte River. It has one main street that houses most of the stores. At the end of the street and next to a small vacant lot, there is a dilapidated building—more like a warehouse—with the sign, "Free Food Distribution Centre."

The Free Food and Grocery Program provides a monthly package of food to low-income people. On my way to the hospital, I would see long lines of people stretching the whole length of the main street and spilling over into the vacant lot, waiting to collect food. For a small town to see so many people waiting for food assistance was a nerve-wracking, painful sight. I was surprised to see this magnitude of poverty in the U.S.

Because while living in India, I thought the U.S. was a land of plenty. The Western media always talks about poverty and starvation in India but never mentions the bone-crushing poverty and its consequences—such as higher rates of drug addiction and negative health outcomes—in millions of small towns across the U.S. These small towns are a classic example of the 20th-century "Gilded Age"—an ugly face of economic inequality created by oligarchic capitalism.

Mr. and Mrs. Miller's home was in the most affluent part of the town. While driving through the neighborhood, one sees mansions with manicured lawns and expensive cars parked in the driveways—a shocking change of scenery from poorly maintained, unpainted houses with broken windows to big mansions: glittering opulence just a few blocks away.

Mrs. Miller received me with a gentle hug and accompanied me to the backyard to meet the guests, who were sitting around white tablecloths covering the round tables. At the far end of the backyard, overlooking the Guyandotte River, there was a half-moon-shaped marble patio with gothic columns where a fiddler band was playing country music.

Apart from the family members, most of the invited guests were rich mine owners and businessmen. The food was catered by a gourmet catering service. The food-serving staff was dressed in crisp white uniforms, and plenty of dishes were spread across both ends of the stone patio.

Dr. Morrison also joined the celebration, and we were seated with Mr. and Mrs. Miller's friends. Mr. Miller and his brother had inherited a family mine, and they also owned most of the gas stations. The hot topic of discussion at our table was the threat of the upcoming coal miners' strike.

I asked the gentleman sitting next to me, Mr. Smith, "Why are the coal miners threatening to strike?"

Mr. Smith is a heavy-set, tall, elderly man with white hair, hooded blue eyes, and a puffy red face, indicating his love for Kentucky bourbon. He looks at me, and his demeanor tells me that he is surprised to hear my question, which shows my ignorance about the history of the region.

He said, "In West Virginia, mine wars have been going on for almost a century, but in the end, nothing has changed."

I was surprised to hear him say *mine wars* instead of the *mine strikes*.

I said, "Mr. Smith, it is just a legitimate protest. The miners are most likely asking for more money. How can it be a war? War is between enemies. The miners are not our enemies."

"Well, Doc, in this part of West Virginia, we call it *Mine Wars*," he spoke, slightly agitated. Then he asked, "Have you heard about the *Blair Mountain Mine War*?"

I said, "No."

Blair Mountain is named for the town of Blair, about 8 miles east of our hospital. The *Battle of Blair Mountain* was a violent conflict between coal miners and strikebreakers. The miners were paid low wages in company-created currency called *scrip*—not in dollars. The scrip could only be used at company stores.

The company also compelled its workers to sign so-called *yellow dog contracts*, pledging not to organize. The miners were living in company-owned homes. The trouble-making miners were harassed and evicted from company homes.

The miners were fed up with the harassment and mistreatment they faced—the company owned everything they needed to survive in their harsh and miserable lives. When the miners could not take it anymore, they went on strike on August 25, 1921. It was the largest labor uprising in U.S. history. This just and legitimate strike was called the *Coal Wars*, and the *Battle of Blair Mountain*, where up to 100 miners were killed during the battle.

In the early 20th century, the term *redneck* was occasionally used to refer to American coal miners' union members who wore red bandanas in solidarity.

The Battle of Blair Mountain ended on September 2nd, 1921, when the federal troops arrived. The miners did not want to fight the troops, so the state of West Virginia charged many miners with treason and conspiracy against the state.

Mr. Smith said, "We, mine owners, and our friends and relatives, owned all the stores in this town. A couple of days of strike would vent out the steam of anger, frustration, and discontent."

He continued, "We will raise the hourly pay for the miners, and once the dust settles down, the store owners will increase the prices for all essential goods—a classical example of oligarchic capitalism: *The right hand giveth; the left hand taketh away.*"

He said only one thing has changed for these miners in the last 100 years. I asked, "What?" He looked at me, and I saw a sense of accomplishment in his bloodshot, hooded blue eyes. He said, "The dollars have replaced the scripts. The only time miners can spend *our* money is when they travel out of town. With political campaign donations, we have successfully blocked the construction of new highways crossing our town."

My conversation with Mr. Smith reminded me of Mark Twain's iconic novel *The Gilded Age: A Tale of Today.*

The Gilded Age, the tumultuous period between 1870 and 1900—Mark Twain called it the Gilded Age, not a Golden Age—signified a thin, shiny surface; under it lay the corruption, greed, and exploitation of hard-working people. The era was marked by inequality and moral decay. Today, the concentration of wealth in a small segment of our society has surpassed that of the Gilded Age.

Our present economic structure has resulted in 1% of Americans holding more wealth (a combined net worth of $44.6 trillion, or 33% of all wealth in the U.S.A.) than the bottom 50% of Americans ($3.3 trillion, or 2.5%) at the end of 2023.

The true source of a nation's legitimate wealth is its people's creativity and innovation. One can get rich either by adding to the nation's pie or by grabbing a large share of the pie by exploiting others, abusing market power, or gaining informational advantages.

There is a huge, vast difference between whether the profits derive from exploitation or wealth creation—the difference between a lightning bug and lightning.

In 2015, former President Jimmy Carter characterized the U.S. as an "oligarchy with unlimited political bribery" following the 2010 *Citizens United v. FEC* Supreme Court decision, which removed limits on donations to political campaigns.

In the French socialist Pierre Bourdieu's book *Distinction*, he writes that we now have two types of capitalists:

Economic capitalists use their resources—wealth—to amass prestige and power; with this unfettered power, they buy the politicians and change the nation's laws. These laws build an economic infrastructure that favors them to amass more wealth.

The other type of capitalists are symbolic capitalists. These capitalists are people from the educated class and the cultural elites; they use their resources, beliefs, fancy degrees, and linguistic abilities to amass prestige, power, and money. The elites gain their status by exploiting or not seeing those below them.

The lesson for the educated class is to seriously reform the system we have created, or be prepared to be run over.
— "Sins of the Educated Class," by David Brooks

As W.E.B. Du Bois wrote, "The liberal elites use social justice issues to build status and make themselves feel good while ultimately offering up little more than symbolic gestures and platitudes to redress the material harm that they decry and often exacerbate."

In 1867, Karl Marx's *Capital* was published in Germany. *Capital* had been in the making with Karl Marx to clinch an argument that capitalism has a specific contraindication that makes it unsustainable, and that it would self-destruct after creating a basis for something better. In *Capital*, Karl Marx argues that capitalism makes the relationship between people and things—and relationships among people—extremely unnatural and incompatible with human flourishing.

Economic inequality is the unequal distribution of income and opportunity between different groups in society. People are trapped in poverty with little chance of climbing up the economic ladder.

It is a matter of time; capitalism, as we know it, will be destroyed from within. Over time, economic inequality will dismantle the present capitalist infrastructure. Whether this will happen peacefully through our legislative framework or through revolution is the topic of speculation. Joseph Schumpeter called it "creative destruction"—when new entrepreneurial innovations arise and subsequently cause the old ways of doing things to disappear.

Milton Friedman wrote *Capitalism and Freedom* in 1962. In it, he argues that present capitalism is a necessary condition for political freedom. However, the capitalists, with their unlimited contributions to political campaigns, have corrupted our political and personal freedom.

One person's freedom is another person's unfreedom. As Isaiah Berlin put it: "Freedom for the wolves has often meant death to the sheep."

Present capitalism has hijacked our political system, and the time has come for the nation to ask one searching, overarching question: How much is enough?

EPILOGUE

The Beggar Boy is about the struggle of India and the Beggar Boy's family to survive the misfortunes brought on by the partition of India. Despite the best efforts of the British Empire to show the world that Indians were not capable of taking care of their country, India survived as a vibrant, secular, and democratic nation.

Since independence, while developing economically, India is reviving its core religion—Hinduism—and mythology.

It has been more than 30 years since I lived and cared for my patients in this beautiful rural town. The people living here are God-fearing, simple, and hard-working.

Because of the lack of money to buy equipment, I could not provide my patients with high-intensity interventional cardiac care. I concentrated on giving them low-intensity preventive and non-invasive cardiac care. We started a state-of-the-art non-invasive cardiac center, and our hospital became a referral center for surrounding small clinics. With generous donations from the mine owners, we bought more respirators and extended services to patients recuperating in the "Happy Cabin Rehab."

I never expected that the most meaningful experiences in my life would come from working in a small town. With limited resources, I was able to help my patients, and to this day, I thank God that I did not walk out of their lives without completing my mission.

Cardiac mortality dropped, and most of the patients were treated locally, surrounded by loved ones. The referral to big city hospitals dropped precipitously. We achieved meaningful success in getting patients to maintain good health.

Good health is about the reasons one wishes to be alive.

Dr. Morrison's son, a cardiologist practicing in Charleston, visited my cardiac laboratory and was impressed. His dad convinced him to come back and join me.

During our meeting, I remember Dr. Morrison's poetic argument: "Son, Dr. B and I are getting old. We need someone to keep the flame burning, and you are the person who should do it."

Dr. Morrison's son joined me; it was Godsent help. The old age and ravages of time caused extensive damage to my knees. Over time, walking and negotiating the hilly terrain became extremely painful and challenging.

The anxiety of becoming disabled and not being able to take care of patients started creeping into my mind. I would wake up in the middle of the night, worrying about my disability, not knowing what was waiting around the corner, and how my life journey would end.

How much suffering was in store for me before the "Last Station" arrives?

All these years, I have been living alone and caring for myself. I had no siblings living in the U.S.; my brother and two sisters were still living in India. My brother owned land in the city of Rishikesh, on the bank of the holy river Ganges.

The fear of not living up to expectations and becoming a burden on society became a debilitating force that compelled me to think and plan. My demanding job was the anchor holding me to this town, and to unmoor myself, I decided to resign to think clearly about my options.

When Dr. Morrison learned that I had resigned, he was upset because all these years we had been working together, and he was shocked to learn about my resignation from his son.

Dr. Morrison asked, "Why did you resign?"

I said, "Dr. Morrison, a long time back, I came to this beautiful place with a mission. I did my job, if God allowed me. Now I am disabled, and in due course of time, I will not be able to do my job properly. So, the right time is now to say goodbye and move on."

Dr. Morrison said, "Bhikshu, you made the most important life-changing decision out of fear of the unknown. You have given the best years of your life taking care of the people of our town. If ever the time comes when you cannot take care of yourself, we will make sure that you get all the help you need."

After a brief pause, he looked at me, and from my demeanor, he figured out that I would not change my mind. He asked what my plans were and where I would be retiring. I said I was planning to go back to India. He was surprised to hear this because he thought I was returning to New York or another big town. He asked, "Why India?"

When I told him about my plan to start a small clinic in Rishikesh, located on the bank of the Holy River Ganges—where my brother owned a piece of land—and my deep, burning desire to follow the Hindus' ritual after death: cremation and scattering of ashes in the Holy River Ganges.

I saw a unique kind of respect in his eyes, and his demeanor changed. He got up from his chair, came around the desk, gave me a brotherly hug, and said, "We are going to give you the most elaborate Bon Voyage party the town has ever seen."

I migrated to the U.S. as a young man, and now I have reached the sunset of my life. I still believe in the Hindu rituals of death, and deep down at the core of my consciousness, I feel that these rituals are the link that will connect me with my ancestors.

As we age, thinking about our mortality tenderizes us. I could not help but remember the following poem:

The Gardener: Peace, My Heart
by Rabindranath Tagore

Peace, my heart, let the time for
the parting be sweet.
Let it not be death but completeness.
Let love melt into memory and pain into songs.
Let the flight through the sky end
in the folding of the wings, the nest.
Let the last touch of your hands be
gentle like the flower of the night.
Stand still, O Beautiful End, for a
moment, and say your last words in silence.
I bow to you and hold up my lamp
to light you on your way.

Acknowledgments

Special thanks to *Mr. Khem Babbar*,
my brother-in-law, for helping me negotiate
the intricacies of the digital world and
for helping me design the book cover

Thank you to my staff
for their unconditional love, care,
and dedication to all our patients.

www.ingramcontent.com/pod-product-compliance
Lightning Source LLC
LaVergne TN
LVHW020713110826
845149LV00012B/2240

* 9 7 8 1 9 6 6 2 3 5 1 2 5 *